The
Barry Locomotive
Phenomenon

The
Barry Locomotive Phenomenon

Francis Blake & Peter Nicholson

Foulis

Haynes

ISBN 0 86093 410 1

A FOULIS-OPC Railway Book

© 1987 F. Blake, P.D. Nicholson & Haynes Publishing Group

British Library Cataloguing in Publication Data
Blake, Francis
    The Barry phenomenon.
    1. Woodham Brothers   2. Locomotives—Wales—
Barry (South Glamorgan)
    I. Title   II. Nicholson, Pete
    625.2'61'0941   TJ603.4.G7
    ISBN 0-86093-410-1

Library of Congress catalog card number
87-81700

Published by:
Haynes Publishing Group
Sparkford, Near Yeovil, Somerset. BA22 7JJ

Haynes Publications Inc.
861 Lawrence Drive, Newbury Park, California 91320, USA

Title page: The locomotive that started it all, No. 43924, a former Midland Railway 4F class 0-6-0 was the first of more than 200 locomotives that were eventually purchased from Messrs Woodham Bros Ltd of Barry Docks over the next 20 years. Acquired by the Midland 4F Preservation Society it was moved to the Keighley & Worth Valley Railway in September 1968. The scene here, showing No. 43924 arriving at Oakworth with the 17.47 Keighley – Oxenhope train on 3rd July 1983, illustrates the very high standards being reached by the railway preservation movement today. (Tom Heavyside)

CONTENTS

Foreword

To most people the name 'Barry' brings to mind only a vague picture: perhaps of an unlikely, even uneasy, combination of a seaside resort for the miners of South Wales, hard by dock installations handling the very coal dug by those same men. Perhaps, as a young Englishman based in Cardiff soon after leaving school at the tender age of 18, my memories of Barry are tinged with romance, lost youth and the enjoyment of rough pleasures that may have escaped my contemporaries. That was 1953.

My more recent memories of Barry are rather different. The docks are nearly derelict, today's miners all have cars, many of the valley lines are closed, and the pannier and 0-6-2 tanks that hauled endless rakes of non-corridor stock from Treherbert, Trehafod, Treforest, are but a memory. Or, are they . . .?

Francis Blake and Peter Nicholson remind us, should it be necessary, of the quite extraordinary link, uniquely provided at Dai Woodham's Barry Scrapyard, between near-forgotten memories of Britain's steam locomotives, and the visible, tangible, actual survival of hard metal from Swindon and Eastleigh, Crewe and Derby, to name but four.

More than 200 former British Railways steam locomotives have 'escaped' from Barry Scrapyard. Many have been rescued by dint of almost superhuman fund-raising schemes, yet buying an engine is but the start. A GWR 28xx plus tender, weighing in excess of 115 tons, is no mere decoration for the mantelpiece! Movement, stabling and permanent residence must all be secured – then the long task of restoration can begin. Over a period of 20 years, 'customers' have now been found for more than 200 locomotives – a gargantuan task indeed. Organisation, argument, jealousy, strong emotions have been aroused, numerous conflicts have arisen. Those of us associated with Barry have at times been described as rogues, fools and much else besides!

Much of the tale of Barry has been told before, but like all good stories is enriched by embellishment, savoured by repetition and enjoyed by those *aficionados* who form the army of the Brotherhood of Steam. Somehow, as t The Barry Locomotives rusted away, whilst the gleam of rescued and restored engines grew ever yet brighter, the poignancy increased. As the Bluebells, the Mid-Hants, the Severn Valleys prospered and increasingly emerged as features in the brochures of the regional tourist boards, those of us drawn to Barry came to regard Woodhams as the true repository of the spirit of the *real* railway that we remembered in the 'fifties and 'sixties. It is this spirit that The Barry Locomotive Phenomenon seeks to encapsulate, combining those two elements essential for the satisfaction of enthusiasts, namely the provision of facts in abundance and the milking of the imagination through word and picture.

My connection with Barry and with Dai Woodham has certainly enriched my life, both through visible and physical contact with *real* engines and indeed through personal contacts with so many people. I doubt whether any scrapyard has ever attracted so many 'visitors' – most uninvited, many unwelcome, some common thieves. Through it all Dai Woodham has stoically smiled and earned himself, rightly, an immortal page in the record book of the history of the British steam locomotive. As President of Barry Rescue it has been my privilege to come to know Dai well. Let it be said – without his tolerance, patience and goodwill the

Barry story would have been stillborn. His acquiescence in the fulfilment of my dream of creating the Wales Railway Centre, aided by Francis Blake, has seen this project off the drawing-board and, as I write these words, into reality. That public bodies as august as the Welsh Development Agency, Welsh Industrial & Maritime Museum, South Glamorgan County Council and the Welsh Office itself, with active support from former Secretary of State Nicholas Edwards, his Ministerial colleagues, and from his successor Peter Walker, the Wales Railway Centre, in its birth, puts Barry firmly into the public arena in South Wales. Indeed I hope that Dai and Francis keep our correspondence safe. If the Wales Railway Centre becomes the success of which I dream, credit will doubtless be claimed by those who came later to the project! Let it be stated clearly beyond peradventure that it was the spirit of Barry that fostered the project.

Many and famous are the names associated with Barry, but it is those forlorn, near-forgotten once-despised engines that emboldened the spirit, enriched the memory and finally galvanised so many of us. They are the heroes and this book rightly accords them their due accolade.

Robert Adley M.P.

35029	Ellerman Lines	104	48624		153	80150	35, 150, 180
41312		102	53808		25, 150	80151	109
41313		14, 192, CP	53809		82. 146, 149	92085	86, 138, 144, CP
42765		90	61264		115	92134	126, 148
42859		55, 140	71000	Duke of Gloucester	83, 173	92207	126, 154
42968		98, 137	73082	Camelot	85, 135, CP	92212	136
43924		90, 2	73096		126, 129	92214	142, 148
44123		57, 153, CP	73129		98	92219	63, 171
44422		117	73156		126, 129, 175	92240	125, 163
44901		126, 180, CP	75014		141	92245	19
45163		FC, 55, 58, 177	75069		137, 167, CP		
45293		153, 175	75078		117	D601	Ark Royal	87
45337		168	75079		85, 162	D6122		87, 143
45379		103	76017		168		
45491		129, 138	76077		153, CP	WD106	(Hunslet 2889)	76
45690	Leander	70, 96, 109, 149, CP	76079		104	WD108	(Hunslet 2891)	76
45699	Galatea	126, 140	76084		87, 126	WD203	(Hunslet 3903)	76
46428		136	78018		85, 124		
46447		95	78019		85	99	(North British 27931)	163
46512		84	78022		CP		
46521		100	78059		86, 150, 165	Non Barry Locomotives illustrated	
47279		84, 126, 138	80064		98, 157		
47298		134, 149, 166	80072		178, 180	3041	The Queen	163
47324		124	80078		116	4027		97
47327		92	80079		68, 118, 149, 192	5820	"Big Jim"	90, 117
47357		92. 97	80080		141	47445		92
47406		90	80097		171 CP	D2245		124
47493		113	80098		141	D6584	(33 064)	88
48151		108	80100		124	D7029		148
48173		17, 63, 126, 180	80104		141, 150	08 352		135
48305		56, CP	80105		98	31 295		25
48431		68, 95, 100	80135		80, 147, 192, CP		
48518		150, 178	80136		26. 136	FC = Front cover	
						CP = Colour Plates	

Acknowledgements

We would like to thank most sincerely all those who have assisted in the compilation of this book – nearly all at very short notice. Photographs are individually credited but we take this opportunity to acknowledge the following for the supply of information and selections of photographs.

M. J. Allen, D. J. Andrews, J. Arkell, M. Ashworth, M. J. Beckett, J. H. Bird, M. Cokayne, S. Edge, R. Elliott, J. Graham, R. C. Hardingham, T. Heavyside, P. Hebson, D. Howells, D. A.Idle, M. Lawrence, H. Lee, P. Lyons, E. Miller, R. Nattress, A. Pearson, J. B. Radford, D. Sartin, G. Scott-Lowe, R. Sim, A. Wakefield, D. & N. Ward, S. Whittaker, D. Wilcock, S. Worrall and D. L. V. Woodham BEM, MBE.

Thanks are also due to those who supplied quotes and photographs for the chapter 'Why They Got Involved'.

Abbreviations

The use of abbreviations has been kept to a minimum in general, but for space considerations, particularly when referring to railway companies the following have been used:

BR	British Railways/British Rail
BREL	British Rail Engineering Limited
BRM	Birmingham Railway Museum
BSLAG	Barry Steam Locomotive Action Group
BTSR	Buckfastleigh & Totnes Steam Railway
BWR	Bodmin & Wenford Railway
CWR	Cholsey & Wallingford Railway
DFR	Dean Forest Railway
dmu	diesel multiple unit
DVR	Dart Valley Railway
ecs	empty carriage stock
ELR	East Lancashire Railway
ESR	East Somerset Railway
GCR	Great Central Railway Company (1976) Limited
GW/GC	Great Western & Great Central Railway Joint Line
GWR	Great Western Railway
G-WR	Gloucestershire Warwickshire Railway
GWSLG	Great Western Steam Locomotives Group
GWRPG	GWR Preservation Group
GWS	Great Western Society
KWVR	Keighley & Worth Valley Railway
LBSCR	London, Brighton & South Coast Railway
LHR	Lakeside & Haverthwaite Railway
LMSR	London, Midland & Scottish Railway
LNER	London & North Eastern Railway
LSVR	Lower Swansea Valley Railway
LSWR	London & South Western Railway
LT	London Transport
MAG	Midlands Action Group
MHR	Mid-Hants Railway
MRC	Midland Railway Centre
MSC	Manpower Services Commission
NCB	National Coal Board
NRM	National Railway Museum
NRPC	National Railway Preservation Campaign
NSR	North Staffordshire Railway Society
NVR	Nene Valley Railway
NYMR	North Yorkshire Moors Railway
PDSR	Paignton & Dartmouth Steam Railway
PRS	Peak Railway Society
PVR	Plym Valley Railway
S & D	Somerset & Dorset
SAR	South African Railways
SCR	Swindon & Cricklade Railway
SR	Southern Railway
SRPS	Scottish Railway Preservation Society
SVR	Severn Valley Railway
TDR	Torbay & Dartmouth Railway
WRC	Wales Railway Centre
WSR	West Somerset Railway
YDR	Yorkshire Dales Railway

Introduction

Barry means different things to different people. The name has become synonymous with the extensive railway dismantling yard of Messrs Woodham Bros, which has put this once thriving and prosperous South Wales port on the map more significantly than anything previously.

For many it has become a magic name, conjuring up an unbelievable opportunity to acquire a former British Railways' steam locomotive and is no less than a dream come true. Others look upon the whole phenomenon as nothing more than a distraction and a bottomless pit, swallowing up all available finance and effort in detriment to the original railway preservation movement. Therefore, while some realise it has been the saviour of steam it is also seen to have put railway preservation into a much wider sphere of influence and importance – no longer is it just for a few dedicated eccentrics.

This book aims to show something of what a fantastic opportunity has been presented, and taken, by a very large number of people from all walks of life. Perhaps no other nation in the world could produce so much dedication, enthusiasm, enterprise and skill for which the ultimate return is anything but financial gain. When the illustrations of rusting hulks, that were once proud locomotives, are compared with those of machines now restored to their former glory, this achievement is brought into focus.

Many of the locomotive 'rescue' attempts as they have become known, are initiated by individuals with a vision to acquire an engine destined for destruction and bring it back to life. Along the way many other people, providing practical advice, experience, finance and technical skills are attracted to the project and join in, usually paying for the privilege. Few who have placed the original appeal advertisements in the railway press could really have visualised the full implications of just what they were starting!

Efforts leading to purchase are complicated, involving many people and much effort. Once restored the continuing maintenance has to be ensured and subsequent overhauls carried out together with suitable agreements with railway operators. Therefore the number of people involved with each engine all along the line must reach into hundreds – the amount of print work alone generated by such projects must account for very many working hours each year!

On entering traffic the locomotive instantly becomes the 'property' of many thousands – those that enjoy travelling behind it and/or watching and photographing it performing something akin to that for which it was originally built. So what starts off as one person's idea passes through a hard core of dedicated people to become an object to be admired and to bring pleasure to the public at large. In fact it is nothing short of contributing a major part to society from job creation to entertainment. On top of this nearly all the finance for such projects is raised privately – no Arts Council grants for Brunswick Green paint.

The other side of the coin is more difficult to explain as it perhaps illustrates a darker side of human nature, that of envy and jealousy. The controversial aspect that has surrounded much of the activity emanating from Barry is most unfortunate but has been so extensive as to be inescapable. Criticism of those wishing to pursue their hobby became particularly prevalent in the late 1970s, both in the national and the popular railway press where editors openly condemned any further rescue attempts. The governing body of the railway preservation movement also made no secret of its hostility to new groups wanting to emulate the achievements of longer established concerns. Fortunately many of the critics have been silenced by pure achievement.

Much of the negative argument has been disguised as being of "good financial sense". However, this does not take into account the motivation, enthusiasm and persistence of the individual. The classic example was the preservation of No. 6023 *King Edward II*. This accounted for many column inches of condemnation in the railway press as being an impossible waste of money. This was purchased after much fund raising effort, with money being contributed by a large number of people, often only nominal amounts just to indicate their support. The feeling was that a locomotive as important as a Great Western 'King' class 4-6-0 simply could not be allowed to be lost – just what would future generations think, if having had this second chance it had not been seized?

Following its purchase in 1982 for £12,000 an offer was received from Harvey's of Bristol who also realised its historic significance. It then changed hands for £23,000 – without even having turned its

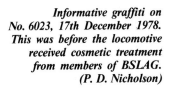

Informative graffiti on No. 6023, 17th December 1978. This was before the locomotive received cosmetic treatment from members of BSLAG.
(P. D. Nicholson)

broken wheels, the finance being used to secure the future of further locomotives at Barry. Under its new ownership a Manpower Services Commission grant has been obtained, so not only is this locomotive, which was more condemned by so-called railway enthusiasts than the scrap trade, being restored for all to enjoy, but it is also providing employment for a number of people who would otherwise still be seeking jobs. The economic argument begins to pale.

This has been very much the image of Barry that has been portrayed in the railway press in recent years – the 'fors' and 'againsts', and finally, the achievements. Meanwhile history has been made, frequently passing by unrecorded in the media and it is now time to start placing this on record. The 28 year period of the Barry phenomenon in fact covers a length of time more than one sixth the total of all British steam railway history from 1825.

Over the years much has been written, discussed, theorised and surmised as to why over 200 of British Railways' steam locomotives should survive into the 1980s. The company, Woodham Bros Ltd at Barry is another story, but their involvement with steam, dates back

A roof top view of the West Pond site, 2nd September 1966. Note how complete the locomotives appear – all still have chimneys and dome covers in situ. No. 3802 nearest the camera, left, even has its cab windows unbroken. (P. D. Nicholson)

Above right: A view in the opposite direction, 13 years later, 24th October 1979 – engines still very tightly packed in but now showing signs of deterioration. (P. D. Nicholson)

to the late 1950s when brothers William and David (Billy and Dai) made the decision to expand their wagon cutting business into the locomotive field – something that had not been done previously by any private scrap dealers. A meeting took place at Swindon where discussions were held with a number of high ranking BR officials. BR's plans for the future were revealed, including the fact that over the next few years locomotives were to be disposed of at a rate far in excess of their own cutting up facilities. Also, the number of wagons was to be reduced drastically – an optimum quantity having been determined for future use – and the figures for disposal, phased over a period, had been calculated.

Woodham Bros placed the first successful tender for the purchase of steam locomotives for scrap in 1959, with Dai spending a week at Swindon in order to learn the art of cutting up locomotives as quickly and economically as possible. As time went by the "Modernisation Plan" progressed, with the complete abolition of the steam locomotive resulting in more and more becoming available for purchase by tender. Of course, such purchases had to

A 1983 view looking towards Barry town. In the foreground are piles of track panels which were responsible for a further reprieve in locomotive cutting, when there was a lull in the wagon supplies.
(Courtesy D. L. V. Woodham)

be made as BR decided, even though the supply of rolling stock was continuing unabated.

It had been stated that once the wagon fleet had been reduced to a certain level, disposal would ease off. Therefore Woodham's kept the locomotives in reserve, waiting for this slack period. What no one realised at the time was the immense impact the introduction of mechanised handling was going to have on industry and its "knock on" effect on the rail system. Containers, pallets and fork lift trucks, and then the computerisation of warehouses, all favoured road haulage. Coupled with the Government policy to extend motorways, which were unquestionably needed to handle this traffic, all led to an ever decreasing requirement for rolling stock.

Even the rolling stock it was intended to keep has had to be superseded with more efficient vehicles carrying block loads. Since the 1950s, all through the '60s and '70s and even into the '80s, British Rail has continued to dispose of wagons at a phenomenal rate. At one time Woodham's sidings were filled with wooden bodied coal

trucks. These became replaced by steel sided mineral wagons, while today, relatively modern stock lines the sidings in the docks, all awaiting attention in their yard. The wagons have never stopped coming. In early 1987 the cutting yard was filled with BR Standard brake vans – no longer required on the fully fitted freight trains of today.

Every month witnesses the arrival of trains of rolling stock in the reception sidings. Barry has proved to be the ideal location for this work as the tracks, once busy with coal wagons are now used to store discarded stock awaiting the torch in Woodham's yard. The deregulation of scrap and entry into the EEC has lifted export restrictions so that scrap metal can be loaded straight onto ships destined for such places as Spain.

There is no mystery or long term scheming behind the retention of the steam locomotives, as much as people may wish to think so. It has simply been a matter of financial consideration coupled with working practices, and not that the locomotives themselves have been looked upon as an 'investment'. Wagons are much easier and quicker to reduce to saleable metal for reprocessing, and most of the time there have been more than enough to keep the work force employed. On the odd occasion when there has been an interruption in supplies, there has been no hesitation in bringing a locomotive or two into the cutting up area and disposing of it. This happened in 1980 and it was only the intervention of the annual holiday that put a stop to any further locomotives being cut up, as in the meantime a further supply of wagons was obtained.

The revenue produced from the sale of each locomotive, even a large one, is negligible compared with a week's through-put of rolling stock. Also, if they can be sold without having to pay someone to spend time cutting them into pieces, all the better. Although the price of locomotives sold intact did go up quite steeply in the mid to late 1970s, since then prices have remained fairly constant and even went down at one time.

Something that is rarely considered is that the land is leased from Associated British Ports and the area occupied by each locomotive can be calculated in rental terms, but this has never been taken into account when arriving at prices. (All locomotives have had their prices worked out from well thumbed copies of Ian Allan ABC Books, constantly on Dai's desk!). On many occasions engines have been sold and then remained on site for a number of years but again no rent has been levied.

The work must go on! A wagon is reduced to scrap in the cutting up area, this being Woodham's main source of revenue. In the background is No. 45163, ready for winching onto road transport, 12th January 1987.
(P. D. Nicholson)

A further 'knock' at the investment theory is the comparison in cash value 1960s – 1980s. For example the £1,450 paid by Woodham's in 1964 for a 4-6-0, if otherwise 'invested' would today be worth at least £13,000 – far in excess of the price of any locomotive sold by them.

Meetings with BR have never resulted in accurate figures long term for their wagon fleet reduction and it has nearly always been greater than anticipated. The purchase of stock is made by competitive tender so no one purchase is guaranteed. The price has not been got right every time, just most of the time. The loss of a number of such tenders would almost certainly have resulted in the destruction of the locomotives, but fortunately this has never happened. Perhaps because of this success rate in tendering there are fewer competitors in the field so this ensures that Woodham's still have a large slice of the market today.

At one time bids were submitted for stock from all over the country, but handling and haulage charges are now so high as to make this uneconomic. Only vehicles in the South Wales/Western Region area are normally applied for, but even this reduced sphere of activity has continued to keep the yard fully employed. BR's attempt to undertake the work themselves – another 'scare' a couple of years back, was short lived.

Many will not like to accept the commonsense that has ensured the locomotives survival, some preferring to believe a more romantic view that Dai Woodham deliberately set out to be the saviour of British steam locomotives. Others see him as no more than a shrewd businessman who knew all along that people would be prepared to pay small fortunes for vandalised hulks, if he kept them long enough.

An observation has been made though, regarding human nature. The Company has never removed any of the component parts from the locomotives, other than some non ferrous fittings – such as axle brasses for safe keeping, and these have been made available at no extra charge – to those locomotive buyers who knew to ask for them! On the other hand, as can be seen today, the remaining engines have been pretty well stripped of all removable parts over the years. Most of these parts have been taken into the railway preservation movement and therefore almost certainly still exist somewhere. The price of a locomotive has never been reduced because of missing parts as these are said to be of little note in calculating the total weight for scrap purposes.

Obviously the most complete locomotives in what has been considered the best state have been purchased first. So now it is down to the most heavily stripped locomotives of the worst condition (in theory) at prices higher than they once were. The result is that there is probably *more* interest in the purchase of them now than ever before, with longer reservation lists on each than any time previously! This is of course because the reality is now becoming apparent – this definitely is the last chance to obtain a British built main line locomotive at what will be looked back upon as a bargain price. To illustrate this point, one example purchased from here a few years ago, with its driving wheels cut through and with no restoration work having been undertaken subsequently, has a price tag today from its current owners of £75,000.

The condition of the locomotives in the yard has been the subject of much discussion, often by those with little real knowledge of the workings of the steam locomotive. One point that is invariably overlooked is that these machines were not discarded because they were defective or worn out, but because they were superseded as a mode of motive power. But for this, many were very early on in their expected working lives, and remember, even those missing parts are still around – somewhere.

In the Spring of 1987 the proposals for Barry No.1 Dock Site are being progressed, this being the redevelopment of the whole area for housing and recreation in a multi-million pound scheme. This will mean that Woodham's will have to vacate their site, and although the Council has said that they would like one of the locomotives for display, the remainder will obviously have to be gone soon. The latest deadline has been set for March 1988.

Of the 27 locomotives still present at the time of writing eleven have been sold and await collection, six are reserved for private purchase, with the other ten earmarked for the ambitious Wales Railway Centre in Cardiff. Money has been granted for the bulk purchase, but no decision can be made until the go-ahead is given for the site at Bute Road Station. Mr. Woodham has stated that when the final deadline is reached he will have no alternative but to "put the locomotives under the lamp" and give cash refunds where applicable.

Dai Woodham's personal feelings are that the job creation aspect has been the most important element in the survival of the Barry locomotives. In addition to a number of full time fitters employed by some railways, there has been a lot of work put out by owners to commercial concerns. Also, without the influx of Barry engines to the tourist railway market, many such schemes, which employ full time staff would probably never have been contemplated, and certainly not on the scale that they are being operated today and planned for in the future. The whole railway preservation movement is now so incredibly vast and far reaching in its influence that few people in fact can be fully appreciative of this fact. There are few organisations of any sort that can be even compared with the number of people involved in, and the total amount of money accounted for, in the world of railway preservation today.

Without the Barry locomotives and all of the people that they have brought in, one wonders where railway preservation would be today. In effect, other than industrial railway equipment, development of steam railway preservation would have been brought to a sudden and early halt in 1968, with British Railways' disposal of its last steam locomotive. One possibility would have been a greater number of Continental type locomotives being imported, which would have resulted in a very distorted representation of the steam locomotive in this Country. A few for comparison and study are of interest, and are an asset, but a majority would be totally unacceptable to a great many people, who would probably feel unable to give their support to the furtherance of steam passenger railway development.

The fact that each locomotive acquired from Barry is an engineering challenge is very much part of the attraction. Had they been acquired by Woodham's and then kept in full working order in showroom type conditions, then a very different clientele would have been attracted. Several engines would probably have been lost abroad anyway, while many people would almost certainly have been attracted to an alternative pastime and never got involved with railway preservation. Even now, untouched locomotives, if removed

Left: An example of a locomotive type which would no longer be with us today but for Barry. Ex Southern Railway 'Q' class 0-6-0 No. 541 (BR No. 30541) on the Bluebell Railway, approaching Freshfield with the 15.37 Sheffield Park – Horsted Keynes working, 30th March 1986. (Tom Heavyside)

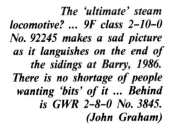

The 'ultimate' steam locomotive? ... 9F class 2-10-0 No. 92245 makes a sad picture as it languishes on the end of the sidings at Barry, 1986. There is no shortage of people wanting 'bits' of it ... Behind is GWR 2-8-0 No. 3845. (John Graham)

from Barry still present a challenge that some will find irresistible. Several will no doubt change hands again before restoration to working order is completed. To have all these locomotives in working order at any one time is quite unnecessary as well as being impractical anyway. It is important to keep some 'raw material' for the future.

The whole Barry saga has produced an air of mystique and those who have known the yard will never forget the experience of seeing and being amongst the endless lines of silent motive power. As one who has long been actively involved in rescuing locomotives and encouraging others, a visit to the yard in early 1987 found a certain sadness as the last few remaining engines, now scattered with several in isolation, awaited their fate. The rescue of these now looks inevitable, although by no means definite. The grass and weeds are growing up again where locomotives once stood and never again will such a concentration of steam locomotives be witnessed. Most have gone to good homes, but nevertheless their presence at Barry will be missed.

After more than a quarter of a century, the day when the last locomotive makes its departure will soon be here, and it will be a notable occasion. The particular engine will secure for itself a unique place in railway history. It would be appropriate if this 'honour' was to fall to 9F class 2-10-0 No. 92245 as this is the highest number of any surviving BR steam locomotive and by rights should have been one of the very last to be built (the delayed Swindon batch securing this status of course, Nos. 92203-92220). We will have to wait and see what happens in the last days, the uncertainty of the future being one of the fascinations of the Barry phenomenon. The locomotives have now nearly all gone, and from there some have already stepped into the limelight, but for others their story has only just begun ...

Chapter 1

Barry Beginnings

New Year's Eve 1947. As locomotive crews whistled in the New Year it heralded the end of the separate railway companies which, with the stroke of midnight, were to be Nationalised.

Although there were no immediate attempts to eliminate steam as the main source of motive power, it was the new concern's "Modernisation Plan" in 1955 that resulted in more than 16,000 locomotives being withdrawn with speed and in volume. Some had worked less than five years, others more than 60, it did not matter, the crusade was on to replace them with the 'all problem-solving' diesel.

Normal practice had been for condemned locomotives to be dealt with at the larger railway works, but as storage yards became filled with thousands of engines queued awaiting the cutter's torch, it became increasingly necessary to find means of alleviating the congestion.

The change in motive power was inevitable, but had the old companies survived, it is likely that they would have staggered the withdrawals over a longer period of time, having respect for the economic working life of the locomotives, and this would have enabled them to be cut up within their various works.

So, it was Nationalisation that enabled the locomotives to arrive at private yards – but it was the efforts of another infamous figure that was to ensure that most of the locomotives that were purchased by Messrs Woodham Bros of Barry were to survive more than 25 years later. Woodham's were already involved in breaking up rolling stock at their site on Barry Docks, so it was hardly surprising perhaps that they were the first yard to tender for scrap locomotives from British Railways. These locomotives arrived in mid 1959 and were cut up without delay. Locomotives continued to arrive over the next nine years and although substantial numbers were broken up in 1961, and again in 1965, as well as smaller quantities in the intervening years, the overall number in the yards continued to grow, reaching a peak of 221 in 1968.

Of the steam locomotives that were cut just four were of classes that do not survive in preservation (3150 and 5400 classes). However, there were quite a lot of what would have been ideal engines today, various pannier tanks, and some Ivatt tanks as well. That was at Woodham Bros, examples of a further class that is now extinct (7400) being cut by another company at Barry.

There has been much conjecture as to why Woodham's did not break up the locomotives as they were purchased. Whilst he admits that the sheer mass of his 'stock in trade' has always created a favourable impression on his bank manager, Dai Woodham lays no claim to abilities to predict the future. The simple fact is that men employed in the yard can, in a given time, produce more tons of scrap metal ready for loading on board ship, from dismantling wagons than they can from the more complex locomotives. So, the infamous Dr. Beeching's surgery of the railway network, and the consequent reduced rolling stock needs, has helped the survival of the locomotives. There is nothing to indicate that they would not have been cut had alternative work not been available.

Whatever our views are of the precipitate haste of the "Modernisation Plan" and the closure of many feeder routes to the network as a result of the Beeching Report, we should be grateful in one respect at least. Grateful, because although it did little to help our railways as a transport system, it did provide us with a much stronger private railway scene.

As locomotives were consigned to the scrapyards in the early 1960s, that was deemed to be that. It was a pity – but what could be done about it? After all there were a lot more around . . .

As withdrawals continued, BR simply could not cope with their destruction, so the solution was found by inviting scrapyards like Woodham Bros of Barry to tender for them. The sheer number of locomotives acquired by yards such as Drapers, Cashmores etc make Woodham's appear insignificant, and yet, in the decades that followed these were to be the locomotives that changed many lives. They influenced the course of our private railways – and caused many headaches and empty bank balances!

More than one locomotive came in to the yard under its own steam, Nos. 9681 and 6619 for example. Others hauled several dead engines to the yard and then joined the ever growing assembly. No. 31618 brought some SR locomotives into the yard and No. 92134 a string of LMSR engines, before dropping their fires. No. 30506 set out from Feltham on its last journey to Barry, hauling a string of dead locomotives. It failed at Staines, but the locomotives in its train, Nos. 30499, 30841 and 30847 continued to Wales behind No. 30824.

The second escapee from the breakers at Barry was the ex SR Maunsell 'U' class 2-6-0 No. 31618. Note how remarkably complete the locomotive is, including motion and coupling rods. The reason for this was that it actually arrived in steam, hauling sister 'U boats' Nos. 31625, 31638 and 31806 from Fratton shed on 16th June 1964. (P. Moody)

No. 30506 did in fact reach the yard some months later. (No. 30824 escaped only to be cut at Cashmores in the following December.)

Until the late 1960s most of the locomotives came to Barry from the southern part of the country, due to the extra cost of transport from farther afield. The first LMSR engines to reach the yard came from sheds in the Bristol area. It was not until steam had been

eliminated here that the net was stretched to encompass locomotives from the 'North Country'. This in fact caught one locomotive, No. 48151 that had been the subject of a rescue attempt by the Stanier Preservation Society whilst still in BR ownership. This 8F was one of the last locomotives purchased by Woodham Bros, arriving in the yard mid 1968 and was successfully rescued by a private purchaser in 1975. The "catch" never included any LNER locomotives, except, that is, a solitary B1, No. 61264 which had spent two years as a stationary boiler at Colwick before arriving at Barry in 1968. Whilst Barry has filled gaps that existed in the classes of locomotives of the other companies, it has not helped the LNER enthusiast.

Did these locomotives' claim to fame lay simply in the fact that they still existed in 1970-75-80-85-? How did they survive against all odds? Why did people become obsessed with their survival? What would our private lines (and lives!) be like without them? Who are the people who have put much hard earned money and physical effort into restoring these wonderful machines to their former glory?

We can see the results in *City of Wells,* No. 9466, *Leander,* No. 5224, No. 3822, *Duke of Gloucester* and the many others that have been returned to steam. But do we ever stop to think what has gone into making it happen? Also, just how much the owners have done to enable us all to soak up the sight, sound and smell that is unique to the steam locomotive?

When it was realised that steam really was going to disappear from the railway landscape, there were urgent attempts to raise money to buy favourite locomotives from British Railways. Inevitably many schemes fell by the wayside due partly to the limited time available, but also because people had yet to come to grips with the enormity of the concept of the acquisition and welfare of such huge machines. So, 1968 came – and went – and with it the last working steam on Standard Gauge British Railways. But those who had strived through the '50s and '60s had proved that it could be done and it was thanks to the example set by these railway groups that interest was aroused. Various schemes for disused lines evolved, again some failed, but by the law of averages – and demand – some succeeded. Today further lines are still being acquired, whilst those "privatised" a decade or so ago are extending to link up with the national network, (doubtless hoping that it will not retract again and sever the connection in one of its negative thinking, short term cost saving schemes!).

The finality of this disappearance of steam from the Nation's railways, was to be the germination of the Barry Phenomenon.

Chapter 2

Gradual Developments

At the time of the early rescues, locomotives were virtually complete although cab fittings had been removed in view of their vulnerability. Even so, the purchase and restoration of one of these huge workhorses was still largely an unknown quantity, and the locomotive rescues of the 1970s must have impressed everyone. To raise the sort of money needed to buy a locomotive is a challenge in itself, to restore it and maintain it in working order is an even greater achievement.

We should all admire those early groups, without them the railway scene today would be infinitely poorer. They rescued locomotives that filled significant gaps in the overall collection, as well as others of less significance in the eyes of the museum orientated, but which surely gave the rescuers and us just as much pleasure. Some of the rescue schemes raised the money very quickly, others really struggled and took ages but got there in the end, and yet others disappeared into obscurity. As one attempt to rescue a specific locomotive failed another often took its place. No. 5668 for instance was the subject of numerous rescue schemes before finally being purchased by an individual in 1985. Sometimes more than one group/individual would seek the same engine, with inevitable problems.

Some of the early locomotive purchases were made by payments over a period of time and left the yard before payment was completed, an example of this was the Somerset & Dorset 7F No. 53808. Purchase price in 1969 was £2,500 with £250 being raised and paid in August of that year. By the following April the balance had been reduced by a further £450. The locomotive left Barry by rail in October, stopping en route at Bristol Bath Road Open Day before completing the journey to Radstock. Payment was completed by 1973. The locomotive has since moved, again by rail to the West Somerset Railway and should be in working order by the time that this is published. Such practice was stopped however after one group experienced difficulties in completing the financial side of the transaction.

Any voluntary organisation requires considerable effort to be expended, usually by a small nucleus of members. Apart from the locomotive itself there is the administrative work and legalities that have to be gone into, often leading to the formation of a limited liability company and perhaps a supporting organisation as well. (Returning from holiday to over 200 letters is fresh in the author's memory!) There are all the fund raising activities from jumble sales

Somerset & Dorset 7F class 2-8-0 No. 88 (BR No. 53808) passes Radstock, GWR signal box on 16th October 1975. Hauled by 33 049, it was leaving the closed Radstock centre, destined for Washford on the West Somerset Railway.
(G. Scott-Lowe)

Class 31, No. 31 295 hauls the 7F and other Somerset & Dorset Railway Museum Trust stock past Castle Cary en route to the West Somerset Railway, 8th January 1976.
(G. Scott-Lowe)

and sponsored walks through to publishing and manufacturing. There are the accounts and reports, negotiations with various other organisations from the purchase or manufacture of missing and defective parts to the very land on which the locomotive is to stand, which can easily be for ten years or more. Then there are newsletters and press releases in order to maintain the interest after the initial enthusiasm has begun to wane, as the locomotive becomes a mass of dismantled components. The general public too, seem much more willing to put the odd donation in a tin by something that looks like a locomotive rather than one that is being steadily progressed but is an unrecognisable jumble of parts.

Steam locomotives lose something of their glamour when broken down into their component parts. Here the boiler of BR 2-6-4T No. 80136 is sandblasted at Cheddleton, North Staffordshire Railway, 31st August 1981. (Tom Heavyside)

The introduction of Value Added Tax in 1973 made the amount required that bit further out of reach by adding 10% to the cost overnight. Some groups have managed to reclaim this but regular trading is needed to make this possible. Even worse, steel prices were decontrolled at the same time, the overall effect being an increase in price of no less than 65%.

The Urie S15 Preservation Group's locomotives provide an interesting guide to the escalation in prices. No. 30506 was bought in March 1973 for £4,000 – under a week before the increases came into effect, which would have added £2,600 to the price. Their second engine, No. 30499 was purchased seven years later to the day, when the locomotive cost £8,500+VAT. An 8-wheel Maunsell tender was bought the following July at a cost of £2,500 + VAT. Today's price for an S15 is £7,500 + VAT (locomotive only) and 6-wheel tenders are £1,500 + VAT, which in real terms makes today's price very attractive!

S15 class 4-6-0 No. 30506 at Ropley, MHR during reassembly. The boiler was acquired by the owners, the Urie S15 Preservation Group, from Maunsell S15 No. 30825. This has been the only instance of such a major component being released by Woodham's. (M. J. Beckett)

Restoration, like raising money takes differing lengths of time – there are those that are restored to working order in what seems an impossibly short time. Those that take ages but which steam in the end, and those that one wonders if they will ever work again. In particular in this last category are Nos. 45699 and 5043, both of which have supporters willing to come forward if the opportunity is given.

Nothing is impossible in locomotive restoration – just more difficult and more expensive! New cylinders have been made for No. 71000, new sources of suitable chain have been located for Bulleid locomotives, new wheels are to be made for No. 6023; the boiler of No. 61264 which after removal from Barry was deemed irrepairable, is now being repaired. But perhaps the ultimate example of surmounting the impossible has been the purchase of No. 30825 without a boiler – the owners 'simply' plan to build a replacement – anything is possible if it is wanted enough!

One locomotive that 'half survived' is No. 35029 *Ellerman Lines* which moved from Barry in January 1974. This was cut (or 'sectioned') to make visible its "workings" – about ten tons of metal were removed from it at a site near Market Overton, Leics., before moving to York for display in the National Railway Museum.

In these early years Mr. Woodham allowed purchasers to replace parts that were missing on their locomotive from others in the yard. This was on the strict understanding that no substantial damage was incurred in removing the parts. This facility was abused, resulting in later locomotives being sold in the incomplete state in which they stood.

Throughout the decade and into the 1980s Woodham Bros have repeatedly warned that cutting was liable to start, because of their uncertainty of securing further wagon contracts. One of the contracts that they failed to get in recent years was for the redundant coke hopper fleet, these were standing on Barry Docks at the time that the tender was issued. Woodham's were outbid by a Cardiff firm but Mr. Woodham pointed them out, still in the sidings twelve months later.

As the '70s progressed the number of rescue attempts became fewer and the prospect of adequate wagons being found to keep the yard busy looked remote. Thus, for the 100+ locomotives remaining unpurchased in the yard it looked like the end, after having survived so long since withdrawal relatively intact.

By this time examples of all the classes surviving in the yard were represented elsewhere – unless one considers the 4200 to be different to the 5205 class, but numerous people felt that not only would it be desirable to save as many of them as possible, but that they would also be needed on the existing and proposed private lines around the country.

Following correspondence in the railway press a small group of like-minded people met on 10th February 1979 to review the options available. After much discussion the outcome was the formation of the 'Barry Steam Locomotive Action Group' with the declared objective – "To secure the future of as many as possible of the locomotives at Barry scrapyard" – a statement that was easy to make, but more difficult to put into effect!

The Action Group needed a "flagship" and found one in No. 6023 *King Edward II*, as will be described, but the main functions of the Group have been to create an increased awareness of the locomotives existence, to liaise with prospective purchasers and with the scrapyard, and to put people in touch with one another, particularly those who wanted to contribute to, or purchase jointly, any of the remaining locomotives. There were disappointments, inevitably, when people changed their mind on the brink of a purchase, but what really mattered was that locomotives were being bought.

The Group decided to take their stand to the Rainhill Celebrations in 1980. Dai supplied prices of specific locomotives and these, together with the current reservations were prominently displayed, causing much furious scribbling and providing many useful contacts. A bonus was the sight of five ex Barry residents, impeccably groomed, taking part in the 'big parade'. To the owners of these five, their presence in the parade must have made it all worthwhile, and for a few of those watching, the BSLAG stand provided the way that they too could emulate these 'lucky people'.

Information was sought on the condition of the remaining

... And then there were none
Sir,—Now that Woodham Bros. Ltd has stated its intent to 'commence' cutting-up the remaining locomotives at Barry in early 1979, it must be time for *all* of us to pause, and consider that the action of the cutter's torch is irreversible and there will be no more British steam locomotives available for preservation.

What is left at Barry, and of these what is reserved and stands a reasonable chance of being saved? Of the remainder, which are fit for restoration? If the ARPS could entice several of its member groups, with people who have the necessary experience, to survey these remaining locomotives and classify them—as worth preserving, possibles or not worth saving—the situation would be clarified.

How can at least some of these be saved? Perhaps by a concerted nationwide appeal by all media. Time is short: it will be difficult, but we will regret tomorrow what we do not try to do today. Let us at least try to get a few more out of Barry—some of the "9"s are too young to die (and some of the "28XX"s too old, perhaps). I am willing to help co-ordinate any efforts for a final rescue, but time is short so act *now*.
24 Highlands Road,
Seer Green, Beaconsfield,
Buckingham HP9 2XN

F. B. BLAKE

BSLAG makes a stand at Rainhill in 1980. Seated, left is Harry 'H' Barber and standing, right is Francis Blake, whose letter to Railway Magazine had 'got the ball – and many locomotives, rolling'.
(P. D. Nicholson)

locomotives, although this differed wildly – "grotty" said one, "best engine in the yard" said another, "condemn it" said a third, only for someone else to say "it's restorable" – and they were all talking about the same engine! Some of this was found to be a 'smoke screen' because it, or certain parts of it, were wanted by the person/group voicing the opinion – but it changed the concept of mechanical engineering from being a definitive science to a mystic art!

'Wanting certain parts' has been one of Barry's biggest headaches. To anyone who knows the open dock site, it is apparent that it is not practical to prevent access by anyone and everyone. Fantastic claims have been made as to the number of people who have visited the yard, and whatever the number, Dai would certainly have made a lot of money if he had been able to erect a security fence and a turnstile. (Probably more than he has from selling the locomotives, although the air of abandonment of the site has contributed to its appeal, as if the locomotives have been discarded and left for nature to reclaim.) A large percentage of these "visitors" just want to walk amongst, and look at, these monsters of what is already a bygone age, but two minority groups have caused untold damage and created unneccessary problems.

First, there are those who can best be described as 'itinerant scrapmen', who have taken advantage of the site to help themselves to numerous bits and pieces especially any non-ferrous metal that could be found.

Secondly, there are the selfish individuals who help themselves to parts from locomotives not belonging to them, in many cases damaging the adjoining parts during removal. Perhaps worse still, from the point of view of the locomotive's survival, has been the cases where parts like smokebox rings and doors have been cut off and left lying where they fell amidst the weeds and rubbish in Barry yard. One can but assume that this was done in an attempt to make the locomotive in question less attractive to prospective purchasers – perhaps the instigators of these crimes wished to maintain the 'rarity value' of their own locomotives?

Occasionally people have been caught and prosecuted, and in 1981 Mr. Woodham, passing the yard whilst taking office staff home, came face to face with a load of parts about the leave his yard. The offenders were told to unload them or face prosecution – they were unloaded, but needless to say over a period of time those parts have found various new 'homes' and have made it that much more

A smokebox door, complete with hinges and handrail lies abandoned at Barry, February 1987. Presumably it was removed from an engine when purchased and a better one taken from another example. (P. D. Nicholson)

difficult to buy and restore the BR Standard tanks.

This ultimately resulted in Woodham's stopping what had been a useful concession. Up until this point in time intending purchasers were allowed to work on their locomotives in the yard including weekends. This resulted in some quite respectable machines leaving the yard and ones that were also in a much better condition to be moved without damage. This was stopped, and although pilfering has continued it has been to a lesser degree. Whether this is because there is not much 'mobile' scrap left or whether the deterrent of prosecution has influenced such people is not clear.

Some of the parts that were removed are slowly coming onto the market, others are still being retained in case they should be needed in the future. Meanwhile fantastic hoards of locomotive parts are claimed to be stashed at various places around the country!

Before it was stopped, BSLAG's Midlands Action Group earned a well deserved reputation for the restoration of locomotives in the yard, in what they termed 'first aid' or preventative maintenance. Their first candidate was No. 6023, which was currently the subject of a rescue fund. Whilst working on the 'King', they were attracted to No. 7903 *Foremarke Hall* which was shunted alongside. MAG started a fund for this, but it was purchased by someone else and they then formed the basis of the Great Western Steam Locomotives Group. Other locomotives worked on by the group included Nos. 2807, 3814, 5952, 7821, 7828, 34072 and 34073, and that may not be the complete list. The way this Group worked was important. They were not restoring locomotives that they themselves were buying, but those of anyone loosely associated with BSLAG. It was soon found that a coat of paint works wonders! As soon as a locomotive was painted, a number of enquiries were received from people who wished to purchase it because "it is one of the best engines in the yard". The founder of the MAG, Harry 'H' Barber decided that an engine was not properly dressed without a chimney. After a few attempts 'H' perfected his fibre glass replicas to such good effect that when 6023 was officially examined the report reads – "chimney in position" – as good an accolade as 'H' could hope for!

Another deterrent to would-be purchasers has been the shortage of tenders. This came about because a considerable number of tenders from various South Wales scrapyards including Woodham's, were purchased by steelworks in the area in the late '60s for use at sites like Llanelli and Briton Ferry. The chassis of these tenders were converted into ingot carriers, a few of which were subsequently recovered by locomotive groups, although they needed substantial repairs before new tanks could be fitted. The majority of tenders that were purchased from Barry in this way were Bulleid and BR Standard types. Those owners who have purchased locomotives without tenders have sought various solutions, BR have always proved most helpful in providing details of known tenders on the 'TOPS' systems in use as sludge/water carriers or snowploughs, although it has been more difficult to trace those not recorded on the BR computer.

Yet another problem for some potential purchasers that raised its head in the late 1970s has been the need to remove any asbestos before locomotives leave the yard. Woodham's did have much of the

The Midlands Action Group, led by 'H' tackling No. 7828 Odney Manor at Barry, 30th November 1980. Also wielding paint brushes are Keith Edmund and Howard Giblet. Unlike the numerous other locomotives they attended to, they have been able to keep this one within their auspices and have brought it through to completion, its first steam test scheduled for Spring 1987 at Toddington. (P. D. Nicholson)

Above right: A former GWR 3,500 gallon tender at Duport Steelworks, 13th November 1978. This was one of a number purchased from Woodhams and other South Wales scrap yards. The tank/bunker tops were removed and the underframes used for carrying ingots around the steelworks complex at Llanelli and Briton Ferry. (M. J. Allen)

loose lagging removed, but some inevitably remained. The tightening of controls on this now designated hazardous material has resulted in further expenditure to the buyer of any of the locomotives containing such material.

In 1979, someone on a working party decided to sleep rough and clambered into a box van after coming back from the pub. It was dark and it was not until the morning that he discovered it was being used as a store for the asbestos lagging that was at that time being removed from the locomotives.

Sometimes it was very difficult for the yard to be shunted, especially when there were a lot of wagons in the yard waiting to be

A newly fabricated tender tank top by Shipyard Services for No. 73082 Camelot. This is to be fitted to an ex steelworks tender chassis. Photographed at Brightlingsea, Essex in February 1985. (A. Bainbridge)

cut up and the required locomotive was in an inaccessible place at the far end of a line. Shunting the locomotives in order to pull out purchased ones ready for departure has often caused a lot of problems. Derailments have occurred as a result of missing parts, although the condition of the track in the yard has not helped. Methods used to release a locomotive have included shunting sideways. When located next but one to the end of a siding the exercise has been to load the 'offending' locomotive onto the road

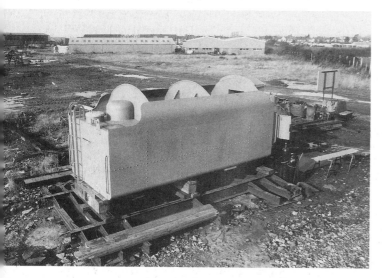

Above right: Left behind at Barry – the sad remains of No. 92207's pony wheels, 25th March 1981. Persons unknown had removed the springs from this 2–10–0 and when shunted to allow the exit of another engine the leading wheels promptly derailed at the first points encountered. In order to expedite the operation those parts off the rails were simply and speedily removed. (P. D. Nicholson)

No. 34046 Braunton all loaded up, 31st May but about to make possibly the shortest 'road' journey of any locomotive in history – to the next track! This was to make way for the extrication of No. 4277 which would otherwise have had an unacceptably long wait for a 'yard' shunt. (D. J. Andrews)

vehicle, then unload it again onto an adjoining siding. This happened for instance with No. 34046 which was moved in this way to release No. 4277 for departure to Toddington.

At first many of the locomotives were moved to their new homes by rail, sometimes three or four at once, but as the years passed the condition of the locomotives was such that it prevented rail movement. It has become a relatively common occurrence to see a heavy road vehicle adorned with 50-120 tons of locomotive, usually with a police escort making its way down motorways, edging through towns and villages, and carefully negotiating narrow country lanes. Because of the specialist nature of this type of work and the purchase and running costs of the lorry, movement adds a substantial amount to the overall cost of getting one's locomotive safely to its restoration site. Transport costs at the time of writing are in the range of £1,500 - £3,000.

Some locomotives have moved considerable distances since leaving Barry. For example, Nos. 4160 and 5637 moved to Tyseley by rail, were subsequently resold and moved by road to Plymouth and Swindon respectively. No. 92134 moved by road from Barry to the North Yorks Moors Railway and was then moved to Brightlingsea in Essex where restoration is continuing. No. 34027 also moved to the NYMR, then to Bury and more recently to Bridgnorth where steaming is expected shortly. No. 7820 moved from Barry to the Gwili Railway at Carmarthen and has since been sold and moved to

The road transport of steam locomotives can cause something of a stir when passing through built up areas. 'Battle of Britain' No. 34067 Tangmere negotiates the narrow streets of Alresford as it approaches the end of its five day journey, and sanctuary on the Mid Hants Railway. (I. Crowder/MHR)

Above right: No. 6634, GWR 0-6-2T en route to the East Somerset Railway, passes No. 2807 waiting in a lay-by on the A449 Newport-Monmouth road, 20th June 1981. The 2-8-0 caught up with the 0-6-2T at the Raglan service area from where they travelled in convoy for awhile, before it branched off to Toddington. (P. D. Nicholson)

Minehead. Another 'second move' was that of No. 78018, which travelled at first to Market Bosworth, was subsequently re-sold and moved to Darlington.

No. 6634's movement to the East Somerset Railway is of interest – the locomotive passed No. 2807 (which was en route to Toddington) on the road, was unloaded at Foster Yeoman's works and then towed by rail to Cranmore a month later by BR diesel No. 47 106.

Impetus was added to BSLAG's efforts when two further locomotives were cut in 1980. Happily, further alternative work was found for the yard, but it emphasised the cliff edge upon which the locomotives' survival was poised.

Chapter 3

Inspection and Discussion

Amongst those that the Barry Steam Locomotive Action Group sought to make aware of the Barry locomotives were Members of Parliament and Government Departments. This proved more successful than the attempts to interest the national media!

The subject of Barry was raised at Westminster on 18th June 1979, when it was reported that "MPs on both left and right persisted in trying to interest the Arts Minister in the fate of railway steam engines ...".

On 5th November 1979 Robert Adley MP asked the Chancellor of the Duchy of Lancaster what plans he had to promote the preservation of steam locomotives. The reply indicated that Mr. St. John-Stevas was aware of Barry and was in communication with the Science Museum to see what could be done with the limited resources available.

The reply to a written question by Robert Adley dated 28th July 1980 said that a working party was to be set up by the National Railway Museum to examine the locomotives at Barry and to consider which of the remaining ones might warrant preservation or provide valuable spare parts.

The "Barry 21 Club" was formed during a visit to Barry before any locomotive examinations took place. This visit was on 21st November 1980 and comprised Robert Adley, John Bellwood (Chief Mechanical Engineer, National Railway Museum), Captain Peter Manisty (Chairman Association of Railway Preservation Societies), David Ward (BR) and of course Dai Woodham as owner of the locomotives. (Francis Blake was subsequently co-opted to the 21 Club). The aims of the Club were "to assist in the final disposal of the remaining locomotives at Barry scrapyard to the best advantage of the Railway Preservation Movement, both amateur and professional (?) as a whole". The remaining locomotives were to be examined and 'categorised' by John Peck (Traction Running Engineer BR Leeds) and George Knight (BR Regional Boiler Inspector Derby), in the spring of 1981 after their retirement from BR. The views of sites regarding further BR locomotives from Barry would be sought and operation "Barry Rescue" would be launched.

The Barry 21 Club would at first sight appear to take Barry away from the Action Group, but was in fact purely a method that allowed those from different backgrounds, who would never join each other's organisations, to work together for the common cause. Basically BSLAG is the Barry engines, and its representatives must be prepared to do whatever is considered will improve the locomotives' chances of survival, including involvement in this type of exercise.

The first meeting of the Barry 21 Club was held at the House of Commons on Tuesday 6th January 1981 to discuss the launch of 'Barry Rescue'. The minutes of this meeting include: "discussion centred around the definition of the aims of operation. Whilst it was agreed that the use of Barry as a headline would catch the public attention it was strongly represented that its use could also mislead the public into believing that the purchase 'intact' of the remaining locomotives at Barry was the sole aim" . . .

The following terms of reference were then agreed: "to work to create an awareness of railway preservation amongst the widest public; to utilise the Barry locomotives as a symbol to that end, for ultimate restoration or as a source of spare parts; to seek to raise funds for railway preservation purposes, including, but not concentrating solely on, the Barry locomotives".

Also with Dai Woodham's help a list of locomotives still at Barry was to be produced with current 'bidders', reported condition, state of funds and BSLAG's assessment of the total viability of each reservation. This was the forerunner of the six monthly 'Reservation List'. Keeping track of 'who had first claim to what' was always a problem both for Woodham's and the railway preservation movement generally. All reservations were subsequently dealt with via Barry Rescue and a recognised procedure was adopted. Anyone with the money to buy could challenge the reservations on a locomotive – the main reservation holder would then have three months to purchase. The secondary reservation holder would not be able to buy until this period had elapsed, but must be prepared to do so at that point in time or it would be made available to the challenger.

Most reservations were made in the early days simply by writing in paint on the locomotive. No. 80150, depicted 29th April 1980 is inscribed 'Avon Valley Railway Co.' but in 1987 it is one of those still awaiting purchase by another party. The reservation list maintained by 'Barry Rescue', with six monthly revisions proved to be a far more satisfactory method of recording who-hoped-to-buy-what. (P. D. Nicholson)

All the locomotives were inscribed with diverse reservations and other graffiti of schemes long dormant and almost forgotten. Confirmations were therefore requested from reservation holders at six monthly intervals and from these a new list would be produced. This has been a job that has got progressively easier as the number of locomotives available has decreased! During 1981 a couple of prospective purchasers chose to bypass the reservation system by sending cheques to Woodham Bros for engines which they did not have reserved. The cheques were returned and the locomotives duly purchased by those who had followed accepted procedures.

In an Adjournment Debate on 23rd January 1981, Robert Adley raised many issues affecting railway preservation including the Barry locomotives, about which Kenneth Clarke, the Under Secretary of State for Transport replied: "The story of Woodham Bros scrapyard at Barry is a remarkable one, which has led to a substantial number of steam engines surviving in the scrapyard for so many years and continuing to be drawn upon as stock for enthusiasts to transform them into working locomotives again. I admire the efforts of the Barry Steam Locomotive Action Group to save the remaining locomotives which are still at Barry. I am afraid there is no financial way in which I can be of help ...".

Perhaps the lack of such money was fortunate! For some the 'pleasures of Barry' have been the struggling and uncertainty. This is proven by those people who 'lose interest' in locomotives once they are paid for and their future assured, then transferring their allegiance to other schemes that are still trying to save their engines.

A press conference was held at Westminster on 17th February 1981 followed by a working meeting at the Transport Trust Offices at Marylebone station on 14th March. However, before the next meeting, pressures resulted in Barry Rescue becoming but one aspect of the "National Railway Preservation Campaign". This was conceived to encompass all aspects of railway preservation under a banner of the four 'R's: Rescue, Restore, Run and Repair. The minutes of the Barry section of the first NRPC meeting record the discussion of the forthcoming locomotive examinations, together with ideas on moving locomotives from the yard to approved sites before payment was made. This was suggested by Mr. Woodham as a means of enabling work to be carried out on the locomotives by Manpower Services Commission or Youth Opportunity Programme schemes, something that would not be possible in the yard at Barry. In the event it was not pursued.

Correspondence from Mike Cokayne (BSLAG Chairman) aimed at a structure more orientated towards Barry. Barry, as Mike knew full well, required an unusual 'animal' with tenacity, disregard of convention, ability to dream and a thousand and one other abilities not present in those representing the 'establishment' – but no changes were made.

At this meeting BSLAG also wanted to know the effect of the report that the NRM would make, after they had inspected the locomotives, with regard to locomotives that were not as technically sound as others. What would be worth saving from an emotional viewpoint is a totally different 'kettle of fish' from that of a purely technical and financial viewpoint. This resulted in the decision that the results of the examinations would remain confidential and be available to bona fide purchasers only.

During the summer of 1981 George Knight and John Peck commenced their examinations of the locomotives in the yard at Barry – an environment which must have been totally alien to them. A meeting was held in Dai Woodham's office on 3rd July to discuss their findings to date. There were a few surprises, including a Prairie tank which had up until now been considered "beyond economic repair" which was now considered "one of the best of the bunch". George felt one of the S15s should be preserved because of its unusual but sound firebox repair. His report records "two ¾ riveted sides extended over door plate to first row of stays … fairly good". Overall their report confirmed the locomotives were not past it – they could all steam again.

The locomotive examinations were completed during a further

The Barry 21 Club and the NRM inspection team, left to right: George Knight; John Peck; Robert Adley; Francis Blake; David Woodham and Captain Peter Manisty. (F. Blake collection)

period in October. Fifty seven out of the 68 unpurchased locomotives were examined, of these twelve were considered 'above average' and 17 'below average' condition. Purely as a guide, those engines that on the broadest of estimates were likely to cost in excess of £100,000 to restore were deemed to be 'below average'. Those likely to cost up to £50,000 'above average', and average locomotives were thought likely to require between £50,000 and £100,000 spent on them. At the official launch of the NRPC on 3rd December the railway press turned up expecting the intimate details of each locomotive's condition – but it had already been decided that such revelations would be detrimental to the cause.

At the October meeting Mr. Woodham related how an extraordinary visit had occurred. The organiser of a locomotive rescue group, together with representatives from the Manpower Services Commission and the Department of Transport arrived in his office with no prior warning or correspondence of any sort, and announced that they would be using a MSC scheme to start restoration of locomotives in the yard! Rather amazed, Dai showed them the yard and then asked the MSC representative if he would permit his team to work in those conditions. The reply was, "I am sorry to have wasted your time Mr. Woodham" – and nothing further was heard!

During 1982 it became apparent that not all the 'R's of the

NRPC were achieving their objective and due to external influences Captain Peter Manisty resigned as Chairman of the Campaign. To quote from Peter's report: "The only real NRPC achievement has been to organise and issue the Barry inspection reports and, thanks to those involved in Barry Rescue, to keep the Barry situation under close surveillance .... at the same time maintaining very close liaison with Dai Woodham. It is important to realise that the total Barry Rescue project relies on the goodwill of Dai Woodham and he can scrap the lot whenever he chooses .... however thanks to our good relations the NRPC has provided him with a clearing house function. The reports, to the astonishment of some, reveal that all the locomotives still remaining in Dai's scrapyard could be saved and restored to working order if the money was available. But the costs would be high, ranging from £50,000 to over £100,000 and even these figures assume that volunteer labour would be used. Much of the money would be needed to buy or manufacture replacement parts. But there is no time limit once they have been moved out of Barry – it is quite clear in the current economic climate that there is no hope of 'National Funds', but a 'Five Year Plan' for Barry has been put forward ...."

The Five Year Plan proposed that purchasers would sign a binding agreement, pay an immediate deposit of £1,000 and the balance, which would be subject to interest at normal rates, by regular monthly payments spread over five years. The agreement to include a repossession clause which would be implemented upon default of payment (the locomotive to be resold, Woodham Bros. repaid and any residue refunded to the purchaser after expenses had been deducted). The immediate aim of this was to get the locomotives out of the yard which would improve their chances of survival enormously. This did not take place and in the event was not needed.

Probably Woodham's experiences with releasing locomotives prior to payment being completed in the early years influenced this decision, although as already detailed, Mr. Woodham was receptive to the idea of locomotives moving out under 'controlled conditions'. The only known situations where 'stage payments' have been made of late, have been where the wanted locomotive has been 'challenged' and the reservation holders have reached agreement with Mr. Woodham to make payment over a period of time. The locomotive has not however been permitted to leave the yard until payment was successfully completed.

It was decided that the Barry 21 Club should be strengthened to continue with all aspects of Barry Rescue with its "raison d'etre" reworded – "to secure the future of as many as possible of the remaining locomotives in Barry scrapyard". (The original 21 Club objective was – "to assist in the final disposal of the remaining locomotives in Barry scrapyard"). Mike Cokayne and Paul Hibberd were co-opted to the 21 Club to help achieve these objectives.

Dai Woodham must have been somewhat bemused by all this, as it is not often that volunteers set themselves up to sell one's stock! He has entered completely into the spirit of the thing, and probably summed it up when he said – "if anyone comes on to me to buy a locomotive I tell them they will have to speak to Francis first" ....

This system has worked satisfactorily over the years. Purchases have continued steadily, there have been a few scares as wagons for cutting became short, and all the time a solution was being sought for the 'last few'. In 1983 attempts were made to include some of these last 'problems' within the Big Pit scheme at Blaenavon, and then more recently as the stock for the projected Wales Railway Centre at Cardiff.

During 1983 several locomotives (including 'Merchant Navys' and 9Fs) were reserved by an embryo company which aimed to use them for a commercial railway operation. It also intended to "raise funds for development work to produce a modern steam locomotive" – but after some correspondence this did not proceed.

Right: Rescued – Churchward 2-8-0T No. 4277 is loaded at Barry, June 1986, destined for the Glos-Warks Railway, Toddington.
(D. J. Andrews)

Below: Restored – No. 4930 Hagley Hall, a well known Severn Valley Railway locomotive. Seen at Newport Rail Fete, 11th August 1984.
(G. Scott-Lowe)

Chapter 4

The King Escapes

Of the 30 'Kings' that once ruled the Great Western Railway, two found their way to Barry. This happened almost by chance, as they were destined to travel from Swindon to Briton Ferry when it was realised that the route was not cleared for 'Kings' beyond Cardiff, so they were resold to Woodham Bros. At the time it was reported in a magazine that Nos. 6009, 6019, 6023 and 6024 were hauled to Barry Docks in early November 1962. This is unlikely as 6009 and 6019 were cut up at Newport during that month, but 6023 and 6024 definitely did reach Barry! Special permission had been given for their movement over the route from Cardiff to Barry Docks, which again was not cleared for these engines to work over in normal circumstances.

Regrettably, whilst in the yard one of the 'Kings', No. 6023 *King Edward II* was derailed during shunting operations, and since rerailing facilities were not available, sections were burnt out of the rear wheels, to enable it to be moved, so that the yard could continue functioning normally. After all, it made little difference because it would be cut up for scrap when time was available – or would it?

As locomotive preservation gathered momentum it was inevitable that the 'Kings' would be high on the list of wanted locomotives, but

Those wheels! The rear driving wheels of King Edward II showing how they had been cut off at the bottom following a derailment.
(P. D. Nicholson)

because of the damage to the wheels it was No. 6024 that was purchased and moved to Quainton Road near Aylesbury in 1973. No. 6023 remained a lost cause throughout the 1970s, but it continued to attract the romantics. The hard headed realists simply looked on '23 as a source of spares and a spare boiler either for '24 or for the legendary No. 6000 *King George V* which had returned to BR tracks in 1971 and worked numerous trains. But those of us who dream (!) could not envisage '23 ending his days in such an ignominious manner.

From the time of BSLAG's inception there was a steady stream of enquiries about the remaining 'King'. Following much soul searching, which suggested a total restoration cost in excess of £200,000 – apart from the wheels – since many, or rather most, parts had by this time been "removed". What remained was basically frames (rumoured to be twisted), boiler (good), two wheelsets (good), one axle with two damaged wheels, and a bogie. However, on the premise of "what the public want, the public must have", a fund was floated for 6023. Needless to say it raised much discussion and categorised the Group as 'mad'. One periodical tagged it "Mission Impossible" – but the Group had an identity – it was "the lot trying to save that other King!".

The 'King' begins to look cared for again, having received attention from members of BSLAG. Photographed 29th April 1980. (P. D. Nicholson)

In 1981 a 'takeover' was muted – this was being developed by those involved with 'Group 25' (described in Chapter 5). It aimed at combining the 6023 Rescue Fund with the 6024 restoration project, with '23 being restored after '24 – but the survival of '23 must have been doubtful. Anyway, the scheme was dropped, leaving the Rescue Fund to continue its fund raising.

Mike Cokayne is on record as stating – "The fund has gone very much as predicted with a great number of people making small donations as a gesture of their affection for a great engine, a great designer, a great railway, a great engineering works, great tradesmen and a great piece of British history. If 6023 is successfully rescued it will be another triumph for the traditional British way of doing things, members of the public banding together voluntarily to preserve something that the massive public institutions have failed to protect."

What was surprising was the way contributions came in from

places as far afield as Spain, West Germany, Australia and New
Zealand as well as from all over the UK, and not just GWR
territory! £1 here, £5 there, regular monthly payments of £1 to £10.
Schoolboys, retired people – the fund grew quickly – it needed to.
The asking price by this time was £10,000 + VAT, so it was with
quite a sense of achievement that BSLAG actually purchased the
'King' in March 1982.

The next problem, having purchased the locomotive was where
to take it for restoration. A site deep in Southern territory was being
negotiated to house the several locomotives that now came under
BSLAG's wing and it looked as if the 'King' would be exiled until fit
again for work. Fortunately, these negotiations proved very protracted.
Fortunate that is for No. 6023 and its followers. In early 1984 Tony
Byrne of the Brunel Engineering Centre Trust at Bristol approached
Barry Rescue as he had a potential sponsor to buy a locomotive.
Possible choices left at Barry were discussed, then Tony said, "Of
course what they really want is the 'King'!". It was realised that
nothing else would do, so he was put in touch with Mike Cokayne,
the BSLAG Chairman.

Discussions between the sponsor, BSLAG and the Brunel Trust
took most of the year. It took some time for Tony to convince the
owners that he and the sponsors realised the difficulties but still
wanted to purchase and restore 6023. Once this was certain, then it
became clear that this was a once in a lifetime opportunity to see
the 'King' restored. First of all though it meant seeking the approval
of the major contributors to the Rescue Fund. To quote figures, nine
out of ten were overwhelmingly in favour and just 1½% against.
Quite a number did want their contributions returned so that they
could use them towards another favourite engine rescue. Mike quite
rightly felt that the sale of No. 6023 must result in BSLAG
purchasing another engine from Barry. The Group's function was
after all to get locomotives out of the yard and simply selling 6023
would not reduce the number still in danger at Barry. To make this
possible from the net proceeds of the sale, after monies so requested
had been returned, required a price tag of more than £20,000.

The successful outcome of these negotiations was that Harveys
of Bristol Cream fame purchased No. 6023 from BSLAG, who then
undertook to acquire a replacement GWR engine with the proceeds.
(No. 3845 is the selected locomotive).

With all of the locomotive's weight resting on the centre and
leading driving wheels, many had said that once released from the
tender, which it was felt was supporting the locomotive and bearing
some of the weight, it would be unsafe to move. Indeed this was the
reason that it was not moved to Luens Bank with the other engines
destined for Brighton. They need not have worried as Swindon had
catered for this eventuality. With one of the Great Western's former

drivers in the shape of Harry Lee organising the movement with his 'boss' Mike Lawrence, the 'King' rolled safely onto their trailer.

Mike Cokayne said that once this was accomplished and they stood in the yard toasting "The King!", his thoughts were "and now let's save the others!".

The 'King' moved to Bristol on the 23rd of December 1984 preceeded through the City streets by vintage cars, drum majorettes, buses, etc, with most of the founders of the 6023 Rescue Fund amongst the crowd. On arrival at Temple Meads station it was craned into the old Fish Dock. At some stages this appeared the most dangerous part of 6023's first move in many years, with the locomotive swinging toward the crane jib as it was lifted. Fortunately all went well and in a short space of time it was safely located ready for the next stage in a momentous career. Seeing the 'King' at the new site, away from the dangers of Barry, it was realised just what had been achieved. If nothing else he had a breathing space and at best he was on the road to restoration – and dare we hope – main line running?

A couple of years have passed, and to quote from a recent letter: "Work on No. 6023 began on site the other week with a grant from the Manpower Services Commission for the first year of the project." So, barring unforeseen events, No. 6023 *King Edward II* will steam again – something that none of us could really have envisaged when the fund to purchase was opened!

King Edward II is handed over to representatives of Harveys and the Brunel Engineering Centre Trust by Mike Cokayne, second from the left. On the right is Dai Woodham. (Courtesy D. L. V. Woodham)

The tender, which had for so long thought by some to have supported the rear end of the 'King'. It is winched up onto road transport ready for the journey to Bristol, December 1984.
(Courtesy D. L. V. Woodham)

Above right: Ensconced in the fish dock at Bristol Temple Meads, Christmas Eve, 1984.
(G. Scott-Lowe)

No. 6023 pauses in the Portway, Bristol on 23rd December 1984 en route from Barry. (G. Scott-Lowe)

Chapter 5

Ways and Means

Just how does anyone decide to rescue a locomotive from Barry? It starts as the glimmering of an idea – and ultimately becomes an obsession. How too, is the locomotive chosen from those left at Barry? Some admit to emotive reasons, but most will state that their decision has been based on examination of the locomotive (especially the firebox) by someone expert in such matters, together with the likely availability of parts for the selected type of locomotive. In fact, some examples were chosen simply on condition, regardless of class, although equally, others have been picked because of their class, or even their number, regardless of condition!

Whilst many of the locomotives had been bought by groups raising money in many diverse ways – such as jumble sales and waste paper collection, donations and raffle tickets, it was felt that there was an 'area' that had not yet been fully exploited. Contact had been made at the Rainhill Celebrations with an accountant, Dick Griffiths, who had happy memories of steam at Reading in his schooldays and who wanted to get 'involved'. Not to the extent of buying and restoring a locomotive himself, but something more than donating money to one of the rescues being attempted. His definition of the type of rescue in which he would be interested was "meaningful part ownership of a loco" and from this evolved what he termed 'Group 25' a method that has been used on several purchases from Barry and, dare it be said, at least one main line diesel purchase!

The concept being that a Private Limited Company is formed – and in the original scheme it was agreed that ownership would cease to be meaningful if the Group comprised more than 25 people, so this was set as a maximum with 50 £1,500 shares. Any one of the 25 directors of the company could purchase a maximum of two shares which could be paid for with a £500 deposit and 36 monthly payments, or by a one off discounted amount – which would provide purchase monies and a good start toward restoration.

Those involved were adamant that whatever locomotive was chosen it had to be of Great Western origin. Various possibilities were considered including the four cylinder types, but the locomotive ultimately selected for practical and economic reasons, was No. 7903 *Foremarke Hall*, a number of prospective co-owners were identified from letters that had been received, a small advertisement in a Sunday newspaper brought in a few more and it was decided to go ahead.

Three possible sites had been identified, which was a mistake, because the prospective owners were divided as to the choice of site. A number backed down, including the three founders, but those remaining regrouped, purchased 7903 and moved her to Blunsdon on the Swindon & Crickdale Railway after stopping over at Swindon Open Day en route from Barry.

The authors, one of whom had stood down from the Foremarke Hall Group, became involved in a similar scheme to purchase No. 2807, the oldest locomotive at Barry. Other co-owners were found both via BSLAG and through advertisements in local newspapers. This scheme also benefited from a supporters association which gathered the monies from smaller contributors and purchased shares in the owning company on their behalf. Whilst 2807 was being attended to at Barry it was positioned next to No. 4277 and inevitably the tank engine was looked at more than once by the Group. This led to a further scheme resulting in the purchase of 4277 which is now safely at Toddington with 2807, making a unique pairing of Churchward 8-coupled locomotives in preservation.

Meanwhile, another of the founders, along with a Midlands born South African Railways driver, gathered together a few more people, again some resulting from correspondence with BSLAG, and set up a similar group to buy No. 4936 *Kinlet Hall*.

Three of those who attended the original 'Group 25' meeting were Ken Ryder, 'H' Barber and Mick Cozens. Ken was already in contact with BSLAG regarding his intended purchase of two Great Western locomotives. 'H' and Mick were being sought by the Foremarke Hall Group, but decided to join Ken which resulted in the formation of the Great Western Steam Locomotives Group which now has Nos. 5199, 5952, 7821 and 7828.

Whether a London businessman could claim to have been influenced by 'Group 25' is not known but a 'Merchant Navy' was soon purchased by a similar method following advertisements in the railway press and recourse to the BSLAG correspondence file. This particular man should perhaps be known as London's 'Bulleidsman', having been involved in the rescue of at least four of these well liked machines. (When stock of these at Barry ran out an attempt was made to interest him in GWR 2–8–0s, but without success! ...)

Another variation on a theme has been practised by Ralph Pottinger who was instrumental in the formation of the British Rail Enginemen's (1A) Steam Preservation Group who acquired Nos. 35010 and 45293 by means of bank loans against monthly standing orders by the co-owners. Ralph has now set up an independent group and is in the throes of buying another engine using the same procedure. Admittedly the loan does restrict cash available for restoration, but it gets the locomotive out of Barry which is all important.

There are also individuals who have purchased and restored, or are restoring, their own locomotives. You may envy them, but they have put much time, effort and money into their hobby.

Keith Bottomley can probably lay claim to having made the greatest effort to achieve his lifetime ambition. As a youngster he sought to acquire a locomotive from BR with limited resources (less than two figures!). Many years later he realised he could raise the £6–10,000 needed to buy one from Barry, and to do just that he got himself a job in the Middle East for twelve months to earn the necessary money. This is twelve months which Keith is glad are

Diary of a Locomotive Rescue.

GWR No. 2807 – Barry's oldest resident, built at Swindon in 1905.

A sorry sight – No. 2807 in woebegone state at Barry 5th March 1977. (R. H. G. Simpson)

Above right: Members of the Churchward 'Consolidation' Fund set to in order to improve the locomotive's appearance – and its chances of attracting cash investment, 23rd December 1980. Left to right: John Longhurst, Simon Offord and David Andrews. (P. D. Nicholson)

behind him. No. 92207, now named *Morning Star* is safely moved to Bury.

In 1979 Alan Bates first contacted the BSLAG with the intention of buying a locomotive. After seven years of 'phone calls and letters he took the plunge in 1986 – buying No. 45163 which is also now safely moved from Barry and is at Hull for restoration.

In 1980 whilst Dai was on holiday a telephone call was received from someone who had spoken to Mrs. Gunn (Dai's secretary) who had suggested the caller should contact BSLAG. Mr. Ryder said he wanted to buy two GWR locomotives, and although ultimately different engines were selected than those originally conceived, Ken was as good as his word, buying Nos. 7821 and 7828.

Dr. John F. Kennedy wrote saying that he had approached a well known line wanting to buy and restore a locomotive for use on

The big day, 12th March 1981. The founder of the CCF/2807 Rescue Project (BSLAG), Peter Nicholson centre, hands a cheque to Dai Woodham on behalf of Cotswold Steam Preservation Ltd, the company formed to own and restore the locomotive – and all that goes with it. On the right is CSP Ltd Managing Director Jim Colley. (L. Ogden)

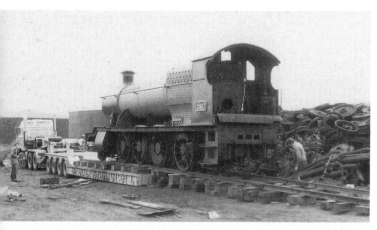

Above: The Churchward Heavy Freight locomotive climbs the ramp onto Mike Lawrence's trailer, 19th June 1981. (P. D. Nicholson)

Main picture: The 2–8–0 becomes the first steam locomotive on the tracks of the Gloucestershire Warwickshire Railway later in the day. Just to the left of the locomotive is Harry Lee – a veteran of more Barry locomotive moves than probably anyone else, having supervised both rail and road movements. (P. D. Nicholson)

Above: The Consolidation approaches Monmouth on the A449, 20th June 1981. (P. D. Nicholson)

the railway, but they were not interested. An alternative site was soon found, John purchased a 'Hall', and more recently, has acquired a Prairie tank as well from the original owners, who had bought it from Woodham's some years ago.

The 2807 gang pose in front of the engine and comprise shareholders of the Churchward Consolidation Fund, the supporting organisation, and Cotswold Steam Preservation Ltd, the owning company. (Roger Best)

Diary of a Rescue Group

April 1980
Reservation placed on GWR 2–8–0 No. 2807.

May 1980
2807 inspected by Mick Cozens (BSLAG Engineer) ... considered a worthwhile rescue so the Churchward Consolidation Fund is launched.

Oct. 1980
Suggestions made for a scheme involving a small number of joint owners ... the Group 25 format is adopted. The Fund will now combine all small shareholdings and donations and purchase shares in the new company on behalf of its members.

Dec. 1980
First aid work completed on 2807 at Barry.

Jan. 1981
Inaugural meeting of potential shareholders held on 25th.

Feb. 1981
Boiler inspection at Barry by Insurance Company on 5th. Bank account under name "2807 Preservation" opened on 6th. Working party at Barry on 8th.
Second meeting of potential shareholders held on 22nd at which share payments become due and company name is chosen – "Cotswold Steam Preservation Limited".

March 1981
The glorious 12th – 2807 purchased!

June 1981
Reservation placed on GWR 2–8–0T No. 4277. 2807 arrives at Toddington on 20th, the first ex BR steam locomotive for the Gloucestershire Warwickshire Railway. 3,500 gallon tender for the locomotive arrives from Barry on 25th.

July 1981
First locomotive working party takes place on 12th.

4277 now reserved in name of "Churchward Locomotive Society".

Spring 1982
2807's boiler and tender tank freed and lifted. Tubes removed, BR Inspector states boiler "OK" - steel stays to be renewed plus a few copper ones. Frames need new section at rear.

Spring 1983
New drag boxes on site.

Summer 1983
Frames grit blasted and painted.

Spring 1984
Near rear frame section welded into place, rear drag box fitted. Tender frames shotblasted and painted.

Spring 1985
Piston rods and missing valve gear acquired and reconditioned. Brake hangers rebushed.
Cotswold Steam Preservation agree to accept 4277, the Fund to be merged with the Company at time of purchase.

July 1985
4277 purchased on 29th.

Winter 1985
Coupling rods purchased for 4277. 2807 wheels have gone to Cardiff for profiling and ultrasonic testing. Sheet metal for tender body being obtained. 2807 frames almost finished, work started on tender. 4277 contractor removing asbestos at Barry.

Spring 1986
4277 prepared for move from Barry over weekend 30th May ... arriving Toddington on 2nd June.

Autumn 1986
2807 wheels returned, springs at Swindon under repair.

BSLAG had several locomotives destined for the Preston Park site at Brighton, but as all movements into and out of this site could only be made by rail, it was decided that the locomotives would need to be dismantled at Barry. With the restriction on working parties in the main site this was not possible, but Mr. Woodham had three, Nos. 34073, 35009 and 45293 towed to Luens Bank where the necessary work could be carried out. Various problems have delayed access to the Brighton site and in the meantime the slightly re-titled British Enginemen's Steam Preservation Society decided to move their Black 5, No. 45293, to North Woolwich where their other engine, No. 35010 is based. It is hoped that the BSLAG Bulleids will move shortly.

A few Barry locomotives have made the long haul to Scotland,

CHURCHWARD 'CONSOLIDATION' FUND

SHARE CERTIFICATE

This is to certify that ....

is registered with ...... *shares of £1 each. Certificate Number* .... *in*

Great Western Railway Heavy Freight Locomotive No. 2807, 2800 class

2-8-0 built Swindon, 1905

This .... *day of* 198

These shares constitute part of one £1,500 Joint Owning
share held by the Churchward 'Consolidation' Fund in the
locomotive which is owned by Cotswold Steam Preservation
Limited.

.... *Chairman*

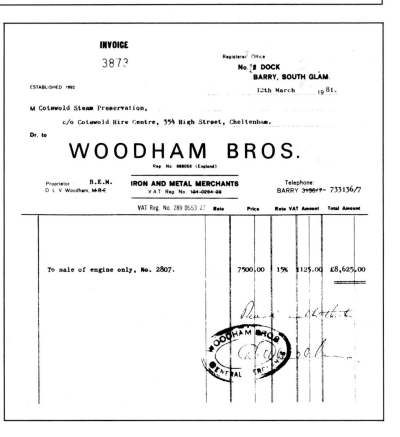

51

Luens Bank 1987. The site where Woodhams first started cutting up locomotives back in 1959 is once again occupied by engines being dismantled. Left is No. 35009 Shaw Savill and right No. 34073 249 Squadron.

Destined for the Brighton Works project they will have to be further dismantled for conveyance by rail as there is no road access to the site where they will ultimately be restored. The building in the background is the old docks power house, the chimney of which is a landmark appearing in a great number of photographs taken at Barry.
(P. D. Nicholson)

some have stayed in Wales, there was an enquiry by the West of Ireland Steam Railway Association for a 2–6–4T and another for static display in Japan. It was not until 1986 that a Barry locomotive ventured 'over the border' into Cornwall, although there had been several attempts in the past. The Bodmin and Wenford Railway took back to the county a locomotive representative of every Cornish branch line scene; small Prairie No. 5552 which had suffered the longest stay at Barry from January 1961 until June 1986. Let us hope she sees long service also on the Bodmin line.

The Plym Valley Railway purchased No. 75079 with the aid of funds from Plymouth lotteries. As there were no BR Standard tenders available they decided to buy a Stanier one. Unfortunately no checks were made until the lorry arrived in Devon when it was found to be carrying a Fowler tender! It was a considerable time later that they eventually swopped it for the Stanier version. Whilst the low-loader was available the opportunity was taken to move No. 34007 from a temporary home on an industrial site to the railway. Access is steep and difficult, the lorry unit failed and the locomotive was unloaded onto temporary track alongside the access road. Three months elapsed – track was laid up the access hill and a heavy road recovery vehicle bought in to winch No. 34007 up the track. The cable parted and *Wadebridge* became a 'runaway', back down the incline and derailed off the end of the track. With a strict time limit the PVR volunteers rerailed the locomotive and within a couple of days it was safely hauled to the site at the top of the incline by a bulldozer. Where there's a will there's a way!

In at least two instances difficulties in shunting the yard at Barry to release purchased locomotives for despatch has resulted in the locomotives being shunted sideways by the owners. The first known example of this was No. 44123 which was jacked up and moved over to the next track so that it could be pulled out for loading. This example was repeated with No. 45337 and in fact jacks were borrowed from 44123's owners to enable the manoeuvre to be repeated.

With the current strength of the railway movement, which shows little sign of waning, those locomotives that did not survive their stay at Barry would prove very marketable today. But we must be thankful for all we have got, doubtless we will still say 'if only ....', but it is thanks to many ordinary people who have put much time effort and money into their hobby, and thanks of course to Dai and his foreman Cliff, for keeping the scrap to swop for pound notes ... a great job well done.

Members of the Mid-Hants Railway locomotive group standing in front of No. 34016 Bodmin, the locomotive they had spent 30,000 hours of their spare time restoring at Ropley.
(MHR)

Chapter 6

And Some of the People –
"Why They Got Involved"

There would be no Barry story without the people who have purchased about 20,000 tons of scrap metal. This has entailed personal expenditure or fund raising in the region of about £1½ million at today's prices. Added to this there has been the much larger amounts needed to bring the locomotives back to working order, although this, fortunately, can be spread over as long a period of time as it takes to raise it.

These people have all spent considerable time, effort and money in ensuring the survival of something in which they believe. This represents our small way of saying 'thanks' for all the pleasure that their efforts continue to give to so many of us.

Names always conjure up 'mind pictures' – I shall always recollect putting John F. Kennedy in touch with William Shakespeare! John is a locomotive owner and Bill the Chairman of a railway. Perhaps the following, which can only be a small portion of 'those involved', will help to make the names that you may have heard mean something:-

Bert Hitchen ... a garage proprietor from Yorkshire, says he became involved with a Barry engine because – "as a past fitter on BR in steam days, a dormant interest was reawakened in the early seventies by friends. I've always done things wholeheartedly and No. 34027 has certainly demanded whole hearts – and finance also". It is really Elizabeth's engine as Bert bought the engine for her as a birthday present! – It is currently located on the Severn Valley Railway and is expected to steam during summer 1987.

Ken Ryder ... a fish farmer from Humberside, well known for his 'Manors' and his associated Great Western Steam Locomotives Group. Michael Draper (General Manager of the Severn Valley Railway) has provided useful publicity for Ken's business by always referring to the "Toddington Trout Farm", when talking of the line upon which Ken's engines are based. When asked why he got involved Ken says "I wished to preserve and restore ex GWR/BR Swindon loco's – Barry was the only source". No. 7828 should steam late spring 1987.

Keith Bottomley ... a chartered surveyor from Manchester, who spent a year in the Middle East earning the 'necessary' to buy No. 92207 which he has since named *Morning Star*, says of Barry:- "Walking around there brought back boyhood memories and my obsession to own my own steam loco. Very funny feeling walking around there, especially alone, not sure whether to be happy, or cry. Brings back memories of better days I suppose. I am surprised they weren't all

Happy birthday! Bert Hitchen presents his wife Elizabeth with her birthday present. The locomotive is No. 34027 Taw Valley now nearing completion of restoration at Bridgnorth, SVR. (Courtesy 'Sunday People')

Above right: Jim Arkell's locomotive 'Crab' 2-6-0 No. 42859 – which his father used to drive on BR, and Class 5 No. 45163 at Hull, Dairycoates, 7th February 1987. (Lois McGill)

snapped up before".

Jim Arkell ... a microprocessor applications engineer, whose father is a retired London Midland Region driver of steam (including No. 42859, Jim's engine). Jim is also closely involved with Nos. 45163; 45293 and 35010. He got involved because: "The people who had it in their power to preserve steam loco's in the 1960s let us down very badly. The second chance that we had at Barry was not to be turned down".

Roger Hibbert ... Roger has been 'prolific' in locomotive restoration! Industrials, No. 5224 and now No. 48305 - he says: "Having restored a couple of industrials I considered I had served my 'apprenticeship' and it was time to move up into the next league with a Barry tank engine. Having got that working I moved into the 'First Division' with the 8F". If Roger's previous track record is anything to go by, we will shortly have a beautifully restored 8F and another loco will have to be found for him to restore ...

Steve Whittaker ... a design engineer of medium speed diesels (Mirlees) and founder member of the 2857 Group, gives his reasons for becoming involved with Barry: "Unfortunately, there was no other place from which to buy a steam loco. It is a desperately desolate place – full of thieving and cheating, especially the selling prices of the loco's which have risen at rates far in excess of any inflation of value-of-metals figures. (Having seen a BR invoice for one of the five 'Castles' at £1,450). What are now springing up around the country are numerous miniature "Barry's" of severely incomplete loco's with insufficient finance, manpower, skill, or knowledge to ever complete their restoration. Sorry, but I'm one of those in fierce opposition to BSLAG, Barry Rescue and the like".

Steve's obvious heartfelt comments show that we all have our own outlooks but calls for the response that whether the present owners restore them to working order or not does not matter, as long as they get pleasure from them and the locomotives continue to exist. They can always be purchased by other groups later if necessary, that have the deemed requisite abilities, when they become available.

No. 48305 has probably been featured in the media more than any other locomotive in residence at Barry. Just who painted the sad face is not recorded but it has graced book jackets and appeared in Sunday colour supplements as it speaks for all the engines at Barry, where photographed 24th October 1979. (P. D. Nicholson)

Above right: Black 8 No. 48305 cries on the shoulder of co-owner Roger Hibbert at Loughborough, GCR, 28th February 1987. (P. D. Nicholson)

Steve Whittaker, top left, on the running plate of No. 2857 at Kidderminster Yard, 17th August 1975 ready to be taken onto 'the Valley'. Below is Dave Sumner, in the cab Rex Butler, in the tender Steve Goodwin and on the steps Bob Kyte. (Courtesy S. Whittaker)

Steve also investigated the possibilities of building a Dean Goods from the remains of No. 3612 (which the Severn Valley Railway had purchased from Barry and dismantled for spares) and a suitable boiler which was available from the Keighley & Worth Valley Railway. However it would have required substantial amounts of money and the idea was shelved.

John Graham ... one of the founders of what is now the London Midland Society, talked about owning a locomotive for a long while with a friend, they went to Barry and chose No. 6695. A price increase put this out of reach (this was in 1977 when the price shot up to £6,500 + VAT (1987 price for an 0–6–2T is £5,750 + VAT) and so No. 47324 was purchased because it was only £4,000 + VAT. 'Barry Fever' was caught again a year or so later when the purchasers of the 'Jinty' combined with others on the Mid-Hants Railway who wanted a locomotive. A trip was made to Barry with the money to buy Nos. 80104 and 44123. The Standard tank had been purchased just two hours previously, so only the 4F was bought. This engine it

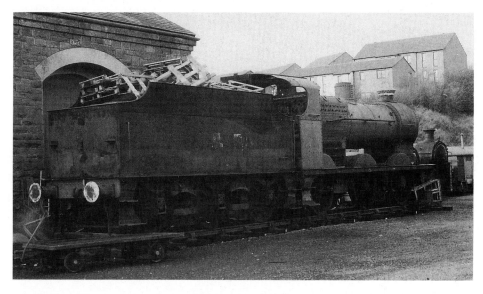

The London Midland Society moved its two ex Barry locomotives and other stock from the Mid Hants Railway to Bitton in May 1986. Class 4F 0–6–0 No. 44123 was placed on an isolated length of track as depicted on 26th December 1986.
(P. D. Nicholson)

is believed, was the first one to be 'side shunted' in the yard to release it ready for departure. Following on from this the Group were keen to get No. 45293, but those holding the reservation purchased it before the 'challenge' could take effect. No. 48624 also had a boiler inspection and the existing reservation was challenged, once again the reservation holder purchased. To bring the story up to date, after 14 years of involvement with the Mid-Hants Railway John and the Group are now at the Bitton Railway with their locomotives and they are currently well on the way to funding No. 48173 which will be bought with a Fowler tender as no Stanier versions are available. John says "I have spent a long time thinking of why I got involved – it just sort of happened".

Peter Weaver ... an airline pilot, one of the three founder members of the Group 25 scheme to purchase No. 7903 who backed down, Peter subsequently organised a similar scheme in collaboration with, amongst others John Gilberthorpe (an SAR Driver) to purchase No. 4936 *Kinlet Hall*. He says "During my younger days in the 1950's the excitement of steam became deeply rooted inside me. A decade later following the demise of steam I realised how much I missed it".

Duncan and Neville Ward ... twins in their mid twenties, one a mechanical fitter the other an electrician who have been deeply involved in the rescue of Nos. 45337 and 73156. Both engines are now at Bury undergoing restoration which will include a tender built from scratch for the Standard 5. "We have always been interested in steam locomotives from quite an early age, although the steam locomotive was already disappearing from the scene. As we have got older the presence of the locomotives at Barry became more apparent and presented us with the opportunity of saving No. 45337 and later No. 73156. We both feel quite proud of what we have achieved".

Dennis Howells ... a BR signal engineer who has restored the only working 94xx pannier tank to such superb condition, says he purchased a Barry engine because "My ambition was to be involved with steam and its preservation for future generations".

Dennis Howells left, the proud owner of No. 9466, with Graham Tyler, and on the right his father, Bryn Howells, 7th April 1985. (M. Roberts)

Bob Sim ... self employed chicken sexer in the poultry industry says, "As I said at the time on television, I hope that 4566 will give pleasure to everyone and to the future generation. 5164 was my choice because she was the station pilot at Pontypool Road and I passed her every Sunday night in the train when I went to work in Cardiff."

Alan Bates ... has purchased No. 45163 and comments, "Belonging to a 'railway family' from Derby I've had a lifelong interest in railways. The challenge of recreating a thing of grace and power from a rusty hulk proved just irresistible!".

Alan Bates looks on from the cab of his Black 5, No. 45163 at Hull, Dairycoates, 7th February 1987. (Lois McGill)

Bob Gorringe ... a company director and founder of the GWR Preservation Group currently based at Southall, says "It was an opportunity and a challenge to bring back to life from the tombstones of Barry, steam locomotives of the Great Western Railway".

Ralph Pottinger ... a BR driver at Stonebridge Park has given a resume of his railway life with particular emphasis on why he got involved with Barry, "My love for the steam locomotive goes back over 40 years. I had great family ties with railways, this gave me valuable experience, for as a teenager I was taught to fire and drive both oil and coal fired locomotives (oil was best in every way!). This was in Jamaica.

Bob Gorringe (centre) and other members of the GWR Preservation Group on the buffer beam of No. 4110 on its arrival at Southall, 19th May 1979 - this being the 100th locomotive to depart from Barry. Facing them, on the left is television presenter Simon Neave. (P. D. Nicholson)

We were taught a lot about Great Britain, so I decided to come to the UK, and seek employment with the railways. I arrived on 1st October 1956 and my first experience was the boat train from Liverpool which consisted of 14 coaches hauled by a Stanier 'Black Five' and a 'Jubilee'. It was an experience to see the tenders being refilled with water at high speed - and we arrived at Euston about four minutes early.

I started at Neasden Depot on 14th October and worked through the grades of cleaner, passed cleaner and then fireman and fired various classes of locomotive on all the turns at the depot -and enjoyed them all, but alas, this depot closed in May 1962. As a result I was transferred to Willesden Junction Depot and had the opportunity to fire the large Stanier locomotives, of both the '6200' and '6220' classes, which were brilliant engines.

I first got interested in preservation when I realised that the plan to dieselise was set to take place sooner rather than later. The locomotives that I was thinking of saving were No. 46253 *City of St. Albans* and No. 6013 *King Henry VIII*, but when I started making enquiries about the possibilities, both engines were gone.

As the years went by, I still had the idea of saving locomotives, this was more so after a visit to Barry when I was told that there were a lot of steam locomotives in the yard. I went over immediately and spent hours just walking around - there were four in the yard that I had fired: Nos. 73156; 45699; 48173 and 48518.

Then in 1980 on a trip return from Crewe, Gary Harn who was my secondman was talking of steam engines and told me he had made quite a few trips to Barry and that BSLAG were trying to save 'King' class No. 6023. My response was, let's join, and we did, and I am happy to say this engine has been saved.

Gary and myself got some workmates together and formed the British Rail Enginemen (1A) Steam Preservation Group. We worked very hard to get things going, and we were successful, the Group having now purchased No. 35010 *Blue Star* and 'Black Five' No. 45293. At the moment I have a small group at my depot and we

Ralph Pottinger – the one with his foot on the rail, with Mike Cokayne next to him. The locomotive is No. 35010 Blue Star one of several locomotives that Ralph has been instrumental in saving. (Courtesy R. Pottinger)

have just purchased Collett Heavy goods 2-8-0 No. 3862.

It is very pleasing that so many groups have been successful in purchasing engines from Barry, and I hope that many of them will return to steam in the next few years".

Terry Rippingale ... who has a computer software business, and owns several GWR engines at Barry, which he is currently making arrangements to move, says quite simply, "I did not want them to be destroyed so I did something about it".

Mike Lawrence and *Harry Lee* ... are well known for their road transport of locomotives from Barry. Most of the other people in this chapter have been asked for a 'quote', but it seemed prudent not to ask Mike for one, else he might turn up with a low loader and the answer "£2,500 + VAT"! So we asked him to describe how it happened. "Harry Lee from Taunton, became involved through the Great Western Society, by preparing engines at Barry for movement out by rail in the late 1960s and early 1970s. He tells me that he has a photograph of himself and his son, amongst others, riding on the footplate of No. 5572, which was, I am told, the only engine to travel via the Severn Tunnel from Barry.

I met Harry in 1976 when I was approached by the West Somerset Railway to transport their three Prairie tanks from Barry to Bishop's Lydeard. Engines came over the Severn Road Bridge in those days and the job was completed in eight days, which included a clutch change on our Volvo tractor unit. After these moves Harry became more and more involved with us and we now refer to him as our 'loading foreman'.

Later that year, we transported *Dumbleton Hall* from Barry to the Dart Valley Railway, which necessitated the removal of the engine's front bogie, because of trailer restrictions. *Wightwick Hall* and *Camelot* also had to be carried in the same way.

In the earlier days, we used an Oliver 80 petrol/paraffin farm tractor (vintage 1942), fitted with a timber winch. It had to be started on the handle and used to "kick like a mule". After that a 1946 Unipower timber tractor was used.

In 1980 I had the trailer, which is still currently used, built to my own specification with railway moves in mind with rails set permanently into the trailer floor. The then new Mack tractor unit was also fitted with a large Garwood winch to facilitate loading. This vehicle has carried out the vast majority of the engine moves and we are still using the same ramp rails that we used in December 1980, when this new vehicle carried its first locomotive. Those flat bottom ramp rails have loaded over 100 locomotives and are still straight.

To date we have loaded and unloaded 150 locomotives, and this figure does not include any tenders or other items of rolling stock. Out of this total, 55 have been moved out of the Barry site by us."

Peter Nicholson ... a professional writer and editor of railway books – in other words an attempt at being a 'full time' railway enthusiast! Peter originated from Surrey, but following a move into GWR territory chose No. 2807 for what was to be a successful rescue attempt from Barry. He gives the reasons that he became so immersed in Barry, "I was brought up with BR steam, with every weekend and holiday (as well as school 'sports' days etc.) being devoted to pursuing them; perhaps unfortunately, more with a notebook than a camera. Although, in reality, had I bought more film, I could not have travelled so far anyway! I could not imagine life without Bulleid Pacifics, S15s, 'Halls', 2-6-4 tanks etc.

But they did all go, all except one rebuilt 'Merchant', one 'as-built' West Country' and a few others – not even a rebuilt Light Pacific was saved. I could not believe it! It took quite a while to sink in as to just how few locomotives had been retained for future generations – and me, to enjoy. There was talk of preservation, but honestly, the amount of money actually being spent to procure items at that time, compared with expenditure in other spheres of 'entertainment' was negligible.

The total number of BR steam locomotives throughout the British Isles was less than 200, many of which were rather ancient oddities from way before my time. There were certainly insufficient to maintain nationwide interest to the degree anything like we witness today. Those few locomotives that did exist would also soon be looked on as 'freaks' by the majority, and the fact that steam had ruled our transport system forgotten.

I never thought in the early days that the Barry engines would survive long enough to make any difference. When it was realised that a second, unbelievable chance was being given, it just *had* to be taken this time around. It was one thing to say that BR had disposed of them so quickly that we had not had a chance but we could not make that excuse this time. The explanation, to someone in say the year 2000, that there were 'insufficient resources' in 1975 to *restore* the engines would be pure evasion of their question, "But why were they allowed to be cut up and lost forever? Did it not occur to you that *we* might be interested, capable and prepared to undertake such work?"

Anyway, we've done it – we've saved the lot, almost ..."

Francis Blake ... an analyst programmer got involved with Barry, "because the existing railway preservation 'umbrella' organisations were doing nothing to secure the locomotives. I have special memories of GWR 28/38xxs hauling long trains on the GW/GC Joint Line. There were a dozen of these still in the yard, and I couldn't just let them be destroyed". He adds "Going to the yard at Barry is always an experience – initial reaction is sadness and a feeling that one never wants to go there again – and yet – it's like meeting old friends, and strengthens the resolve to do everything possible to help the locomotives toward happier times – and having gone away, it somehow has the power to draw one back again ... and again. Although all those involved over the years will be glad when all the locomotives have been found suitable homes – there will be an emptiness that cannot be filled when the yard is no longer there for one to dream and strive for".

Three people "who got involved" with Barry engines, but for different reasons. Left is Francis Blake (BSLAG/Barry Rescue) centre is David Lloyd Victor Woodham and right Cliff Phelps, Dai's foreman. Cliff has probably been involved with every locomotive departure over the years. He will no doubt be as pleased as Francis to see the last locomotive leave, albeit for different reasons! Behind is 8F class 2-8-0 No. 48173, 25th July 1985. (Valerie Blake)

Above right: Frank Vasey, left and Phil Brown prepare 9F No. 92219 at Barry ready for its journey to the Peak Railway, Buxton, June 1985. (Courtesy P. Brown)

Phil Brown ... an office manager comments, "I became involved with Barry because like so many people I had been appalled at the way our railways had been torn apart during the sixties, and Barry presented a unique opportunity of doing something to help redress the balance". Phil certainly did do something, with the help of a few others, Nos. 92214 and 92219 are now safely at Buxton, for dare we hope, doubleheaded 9Fs in Monsal Dale?

Peter Gibbs ... Chairman of the Camelot Locomotive Society and an information scientist by profession, says, "I saw an advertisement for the Camelot Locomotive Society in the April 1974 issue of Railway Magazine. I remembered the named Standard Fives from trainspotting in the early '60s and thought that the last remaining example was worth preserving".

Eric 'Dusty' Miller ... Vice Chairman of Quainton Railway Society explains the reasons behind their acquisitions from Barry, "Well, who but the British, this most eccentric of all island races would jettison good, serviceable machines, take off most of the none ferrous parts for recycling. Then after some ten years or so, purchase the hulks and endeavour to replace all of the missing parts to enable them to function again! 'Mad dogs of Englishmen' indeed go out in the Barry sun!

For my own part I have been a member of several preservation societies since the early days, and with some other like-minded individuals decided that Quainton needed a large two cylinder passenger locomotive. After seeking professional advice No. 6989 *Wightwick Hall* was chosen, fund raising commenced and eventually it was purchased and moved to the site. It seemed only natural to continue and so we sought No. 7200 to round off the collection. This too was accomplished and my one regret is that our founding member and fountain of enthusiasm for the project, Roy Oxendale ('Oxo') was not spared to be with us when we toasted 7200's purchase with champagne!".

Harry 'H' Barber ... an early BSLAG member, founder of the 'First Aid' Group and of the Great Western Steam Locomotives Group says, "It was the shock of seeing the state of No. 6023 at Barry and comparing it with the 'Kings' as I remembered them. All of the engines deserved better, so it was a day to remember when '23 was paid for, and the restoration that is currently taking place is great!" 'H', apart from all his work with other people's engines in the yard, is now one of the driving forces behind GWSLG which has four locomotives in its care.

Roger Hardingham ... explains how he became involved, "I first visited Barry as a teenager in 1966 and although there was still two years to go before steam power was to disappear from BR's tracks, the yard was filling fast with redundant locomotives. My next visit was in late 1971 armed with serious intentions to mark-up a locomotive for purchase, an act which quickly became a craze amongst individuals and groups wanting to own and run their very own locomotive.

Sixteen years have passed since then and almost 200 locomotives have been purchased. What is more, it looks as though every one remaining in the yard will eventually find a new home.

My own small involvement with this unique story has been with the editorship of 'The Barry List', the profits from the seven editions having gone a long way towards the purchase and restoration of ex LSWR Urie S15s Nos. 30499 and 30506, themselves former Barry inhabitants. These two locomotives will join others which have been given new leases of life and which have effectively enabled us to view them at such superb locations as the Severn Valley Railway and the Keighley & Worth Valley Railway.

The Barry story will soon be over but it will never be forgotten".

Bob Hunter ... another well known name in railway preservation comments, "My association with Barry began when I joined the Peak Railway Society in the late 1970s. However, I have been a lifelong lover of steam, having roamed this country and the Continent photographing steam hauled trains.

Coincidental with joining the PRS I found that my career prospects were improving and I was able to contemplate ownership of a locomotive. This lead to me forming a consortium of three PRS friends to purchase a Barry locomotive. My early attempts were thwarted when I arrived at Dai Woodham's office with cheque book, only to be told that our chosen locomotive, 4F No. 44123 had been sold the previous week. Not to be put off, I did some research, and found that BR Derby locomotive boiler examiner Cliff Pegg had recommended BR Class 4 2–6–4T No. 80080.

This did not go down too well at first, as we all had a preference for older locomotives – common sense prevailed eventually though, and I persuaded my friends that this would be an excellent general purpose 'go anywhere' locomotive which would eventually be of more use on the majority of preserved lines than many of the larger, or indeed smaller, locomotives then being purchased. In addition, a more modern locomotive such as this has a boiler perhaps only ten years old, a very important point when looking at the complex repairs now being carried out on 'time expired' boilers.

In addition to purchasing No. 80080, followed by No. 80098, I was asked for advice by several subsequent purchasers of locomotives and it has been a matter of considerable personal satisfaction that my recommendations have proved to be sound".

John F. Kennedy ... comments "I had always wanted to own a steam engine". John purchased No. 4953 *Pitchford Hall* from Barry and moved it to the Dean Forest Railway where restoration progresses. More recently he has acquired No. 4121, a large Prairie 2–6–2T which is also at Norchard, its previous owners having bought this locomotive from Woodhams and transported it to the 'Forest' in February 1981.

David Lloyd Victor Woodham ... a Welsh businessman, said in a letter to the press in 1979, that the "graveyard of steam" would not have been possible without the wonderful, unprecedented and unique co-operation of the British Transport Docks Board. He also refers to the patience of the Docks Police who could have stopped preservationists coming to the site. The letter ends: ... perhaps, like myself, all of the people mentioned derive some satisfaction in helping to preserve for posterity the fascinating age of steam".

It is pleasing to record that Mr. David Woodham was awarded the MBE in the 1987 New Year's Honours list. This was made in recognition of his work in creating employment in the Barry area by providing a number of industrial units and associated facilities.

The man himself, Dai Woodham MBE shaking hands with Ray Buckton, General Secretary of ASLEF for over 20 years, until his retirement in October 1987. (Courtesy D. L. V. Woodham)

Below right: The late Robert Riddles, the former BR Chief Mechanical Engineer, then in his 88th year visited the Bluebell Railway on 11th May 1980 to unveil a plaque on ex Barry 9F 2–10–0 No. 92240. This read "This BR Standard 9F is an example of the last type of steam locomotive built by British Railways. This commemorative plaque is intended as a tribute to the locomotive's designer R. A. Riddles C.B.E.". On the left is Peter Reid, Secretary of the Bluebell 9F Fund and on the right, holding the microphone is Norman Payne, then the Bluebell's CME. Norman has since been involved with boiler work on a number of ex Barry locomotives. (M. Ockendon/BRPS)

Possibly one of the best known Barry 'rescuers' has been John Bunch, Locomotive Superintendent of the Mid-Hants Railway, the occasion was the presentation of the first Denys Fletcher award in 1981. This is made annually by the Southern Railways Group to a person or group who are considered to have made a major contribution to the operation or study of railways in the south of England. The award was made for John's work in saving and restoring Southern steam locomotives from Barry for use on the Mid-Hants Railway.
(MHR)

Most weekends in the mid 1970s would find a number of working parties down at Barry preparing locomotives for purchase and departure. On 26th November 1974 members of three such groups came together and were photographed by No. 30506, these being the Urie S15 Preservation Group, Camelot Locomotive Society and the Dean Forest Railway Preservation Society (top).
(P. Lambeth)

66

Chapter 7

Effect on Lines – and Lives

There are very few major railway preservation sites that have not acquired locomotives from Barry. Although the locations that were in being in the early years were soon occupied by locomotives that had been purchased direct from BR, there are few of them that could provide the attraction and run the services that they do today, without their original motive power being supplemented from Barry.

The Bluebell Railway and the Keighley & Worth Valley Railway have both shopped at "Dai's Emporium", even though they were lucky enough to attract a substantial number of locomotives direct.

The lines that developed later relied on a greater proportion of Barry engines, as for example is the case with the Severn Valley Railway where over 60% of the locomotives have come from Barry, and over half of the Great Western Society's ex BR steam locomotives at Didcot have done time in Woodham's famous yard.

Whilst the established lines strengthened their locomotive fleets, the recently formed private lines have been almost totally dependent upon Barry .... lines like the Mid-Hants Railway, Gloucestershire Warwickshire Railway, Dean Forest Railway, Llangollen Railway, Swanage Railway and Peak Railway, for instance, which would have been virtually devoid of BR steam but for the Barry engines.

Even steam hauled trains on BR lines would have had a reduced number of engines available – several of the locomotives that are well known on the main line, are former Barry residents – *Leander, City of Wells, Drysllwyn Castle* and *Hagley Hall* for instance.

Some feel that the finance used to make these achievements possible would be better deployed in the restoration of locomotives that either never went to Barry, or that came out in the first few years. Usually the locomotive that they wish money to be poured into is their own personal favourite! – but that's human nature. What these people do not realise, and again it is human nature, is that if those who wish to contribute toward rescuing or restoring a specific Barry locomotive are deterred from doing so, then the money that they would have provided will not become available for a project of the deterrer's choice. It is more likely to go towards one of the many demands on people's finances other than railway preservation.

So it is not difficult to envisage today's railways without these two hundred plus locomotives, but it is more difficult to envisage what would have taken their place had they been cut as soon as they arrived at Barry. Imported steam? diesels? electrics? or *new* steam locomotives?

Barry has become a 'Way of life' for many activists. There are

One wonders where the Severn Valley Railway would be today had it not been for the supply of locomotives from a certain South Wales scrap yard. Standard tank No. 80079 at Hay Bridge on a Bewdley – Bridgnorth train, 16th April 1977. (Tom Heavyside)

Below inset: Another 'Hall' which has seen much use on the national rail network has been the Great Western Society's No. 5900 Hinderton Hall. Passing Cropredy on a Didcot – Knowle & Dorridge train, 3rd March 1979. (Tom Heavyside)

The established steam railways have nearly all drawn on Barry for motive power. The Bluebell Railway has found U class 2-6-0 No. 1618 (BR No. 31618) an extremely useful and economic locomotive. At Freshfield with a Sheffield Park – Horsted Keynes working, 9th July 1977. (Tom Heavyside)

Main picture: The Keighley & Worth Valley Railway was the first line to see the possibilities of acquiring engines from Barry. An 8F, No. 8431 (BR No. 48431) heads a demonstration goods train between Ingrow and Damens on Enthusiasts Day, 31st March 1979. (Tom Heavyside)

those that spend all their lives restoring the engines to working order, those that do the many diverse things to raise the necessary money and administer the groups, those that simply spend their time in the yard and on sites contemplating, and those who write letters to the railway press advocating the locomotives should be saved/ should be cut/ should be painted purple/ should not be named etc etc! There are those who want to spend other people's money and those who finish up with an empty bank balance in their efforts to secure their favourite locomotive, but whatever the driving force all have got pleasure from some aspects of the locomotives.

Why did people become obsessed with the survival of these locomotives? Their survival after all others had been destroyed, coupled to increased leisure time and more money to spend on one's hobby have doubtless been substantial features in their survival. However, the major reason has almost certainly been the challenge, generated by the uncertainty of the life expectancy of the engines without intervention by such people. One of the authors has gone on record as saying "Britons are notorious for wanting things after they've gone". The challenge, has been that of making a heap of rusty parts work as a locomotive again, it is not generally realised how many of what were commonplace skills have all but disappeared. Often alternative methods of repair and manufacture have to be found. This challenge too is accepted – and beaten, with various state of the art solutions being evolved. The determination shown in getting over these difficulties bodes well for the locomotives' long working future.

Would you have been interested in what we have called the Barry phenomenon if the uncertainty, the doubt, the struggle, the challenge had not existed? It has created a camaraderie second to none. Engineers work alongside clergy, pilots, accountants, farmers and white collar workers, in fact people of all walks of life have a common interest and a common language ... steam.

The much photographed No. 5690 Leander near Long Preston, 28th May 1983. (G. Scott-Lowe)

1959-1968
The End – And the Beginning

1 9 5 9

9 arrivals:-	3170	5312	5345	5355	5360	5392	5397
	6331	6334					
9 cut:-	3170	5312	5345	5355	5360	5392	5397
	6331	6334					
0 departures:-							
0 restored:-							

The first locomotives to arrive at Woodham's, Barry were a quartet of Churchward 2-6-0s, Nos. 5312, 5360, 5392 and 5397. This was on the 25th March, the locomotives having left BR Swindon Works earlier that day at 5.20am. These rare and historic photographs depict one of them, almost certainly No. 5392, being dismantled. The comprehensive coverage of the process would indicate that there was a certain novelty about the work at that time, and that this was the first locomotive to be so dealt with by Woodham Bros. (D. L. V. Woodham)

Picture 6: A few days later another locomotive arrived. This was No. 3170 the last surviving 3150 class 2-6-2T and is depicted shortly after delivery to Barry. (D. L. V. Woodham)

After assessing the difficulties of scrapping steam locomotives, Woodham Bros. decide to bid for some and receive their first consignment in March.

These nine locomotives are cut up soon after they arrive and include the last of the GWR 3150 class.

1

4

2

5

3

6

1 9 6 0

19 arrivals:-	4164	5407	5422	5504	6406	7712	7719
	7722	7723	7725	7758	9436	9438	9439
	9443	9459	9491	9492	9496		
1 cut:-	4164						
0 departures:-							
0 restored:-							

After an active start only one engine was cut up in 1960, No. 4164 a BR built 5101 class 2-6-2T. However, this was mainly due to the fact that the other arrivals were all at the very end of the year, and none were to survive ultimately.
(D. L. V. Woodham)

Just one tank locomotive cut this year, the majority of the arrivals are pannier tanks including two 5400s - a class which has not survived.

1 9 6 1

20 arrivals:-	4550	4559	4594	5417	5510	5514	5546
	5552	5557	5558	5794	6753	7702	8419
	8473	9445	9449	9462	9468	9499	
21 cut:-	4550	4559	4594	5407	5417	5504	5514
	5546	6406	6753	7702	7712	7719	7725
	8473	9436	9438	9439	9443	9459	9496
0 departures:-							
0 restored:-							

No. 5552, a 4575 class 2-6-2T which arrived in 1961, was destined to become the first locomotive purchased by Woodham's that was to survive. However, it was to see no less than 173 other engines arrive and subsequently leave before its turn came to depart. This did not take place until June 1986 when it went to Cornwall for the embryonic Bodmin & Wenford Railway. Photographed 26th January 1964. (P. D. Nicholson)

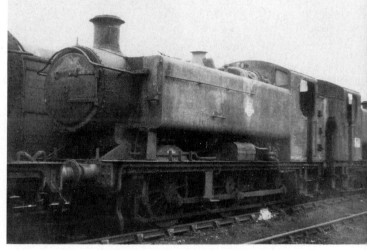

Among the early arrivals were a number of 9400 class 0-6-0 pannier tanks, a type introduced in 1947 with production continuing until 1956. No. 9449 arrived in 1961 but was cut up in 1965, this illustration being dated 26th January 1964. (P. D. Nicholson)

All still of Great Western origin and are panniers and Prairies. Working lives of these tank engines range from 45 years for No. 4550 to a mere *four* years in the case of No. 9499! Twenty five years later almost new 'useful' engines such as this would be 'snapped up' – but all will succumb to the cutter's torch.

The increasing number of locomotives in 'stock' result in Woodham's negotiating the use of the infilled area known as the West Pond site. Prior to this cutting appears to have taken place on the site known as Luens Bank.

1 9 6 2

16 arrivals:–	4561	4566	4588	5182	5521	5526	5532
	5538	5539	5541	5542	5547	5553	5572
	6023	6024					
2 cut:–	7758	9492					
0 departures:–							
0 restored:–							

The largest and most notable locomotives yet to arrive: GWR 'King' class 4–6–0s No. 6024 King Edward I and No. 6023 King Edward II. (R. Oxendale)

Only two pannier tanks cut up this year but more Prairies come into the yard.

Undoubtedly, however, the event of '62 is the arrival of two GWR 'Kings'. Their coming to Barry and therefore their ultimate survival was by fortuitous chance – destined for Wards of Briton Ferry, they were unable to make the journey as the line beyond Cardiff was not cleared for 'Kings' and as a result of this they were resold to Woodham Bros, and moved to Barry following special clearance being given for the line from Cardiff to Barry.

9 arrivals:-   2857   2861   2874   3803   4253   4270   5193
                5224   5239
0 cut:-
0 departures:-
0 restored:-

Three of the six Austerity type 0-6-0 saddle tank locomotives purchased from the War Department in 1963. These carried the blue livery of the Longmoor Military Railway, Hampshire, and are, left to right: WD108 (Hunslet 2891 of 1943), WD106 (Hunslet 2889 of 1943) and WD203 (Hunslet 3803 of 1953). Photographed in January 1964 and cut up the following year.
(P. D. Nicholson)

No locomotives cut, stock in the yard slowly increasing and now including some GWR 2-8-0 tender engines.

As well as the ex BR locomotives, six Austerity 0-6-0STs are purchased from the War Department, arriving at Barry by road.

1 9 6 4

74 arrivals:-						
2807	2885	3727	3822	3845	4141	4248
4277	4930	4936	4942	4953	4979	4983
5029	5043	5051	5080	5164	5199	5227
5619	5637	5643	5668	5669	5900	5967
5972	6619	6634	6686	6695	6696	6960
6989	7027	7200	7202	7226	7229	7903
8475	8479	8749	30499	30506	30512	30825
30828	30830	30841	30844	30847	31618	31625
31638	31806	31874	34016	34027	34028	34058
34072	34073	34094	35009	35018	35025	45690
48431	53808	53809	92207			

2 cut:-	5182	6696

0 departures:-

0 restored:-

The main line-up of locomotives at the beginning of the year. Right to left the roll call is: 4561; 5521; 4566; 5539; 5572; 5538; 5542; 5553; 5552; 5794; 9468; 7722; 5558; 9462; 5510; 8419; 9491; 5422; 7723; 9499 and 9449.
(P. D. Nicholson)

Picture 1: No. 5043 – which became the 43rd departure in 1973, Earl of Mount Edgcumbe. This was one of the five GWR 'Castle' class at Barry, all arriving during 1964.
(Tony Wakefield)

Picture 2: This was the first year to see any examples of Bulleid's Pacifics here – both original condition and BR rebuilt types joining the queues. One of the first to arrive was No. 34027 Taw Valley as seen in July 1967. (P. D. Nicholson)

Just two more cut and a massive influx of locomotives, including for the first time non GWR types, but still from the south of the country. Notable new classes in the yard being GWR 'Castle', LMSR 'Jubilee' and ex Somerset & Dorset 7F.

Further storage space is now needed, so arrangements are made to make use of the sidings above Barry Works.

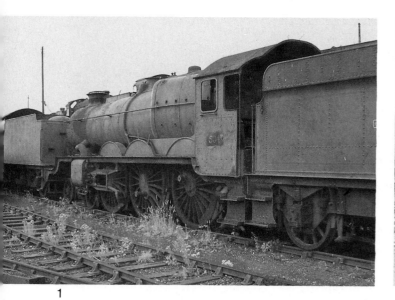

1

2

1 9 6 5

65 arrivals:-	1367	1368	2859	2873	3612	3738	3794
	3802	3814	3817	3850	3855	3862	4110
	4115	4121	4144	4150	4156	4157	4160
	4247	4612	5322	5651	5952	6115	6621
	7325	9466	9629	9681	9682	30541	34007
	34010	34039	34045	34046	34067	34070	34081
	34092	34105	35006	41248	41303	43924	44123
	44222	45163	45293	45337	45379	45491	45699
	48173	48518	48624	80067	92214	92219	92232
	92240	92245					
36 cut:-	1367	1368	3727	3794	4157	5422	5510
	5547	5557	5558	5651	5669	5794	6115
	6621	7226	7722	7723	8419	8475	8479
	8749	9445	9449	9462	9468	9491	9499
	30512	30844	34045	34094	41248	41303	80067
	92232						
0 departures:-							
0 restored:-							

Holocaust! Cutting recommences in earnest, mostly of 'useful' tank engines and the ex WD locomotives that arrived in '63. In some compensation stock in the yard is still over 30 more by the end of the year, including for the first time examples of BR Standard classes.

Although it could not be known at the time, this was to be the last year of 'wholesale destruction' with the considerable number of wagons being scrapped by the railways, together with the changing scrap market, it was a better commercial operation to leave the locomotives until other sources of scrap were not available.

Geography has always determined the viability of tendering for redundant railway stock, because transport costs have to be taken into account, but the catchment area is stretching far afield with 'Black Fives' being 'captured' from Carlisle.

With the LNER so badly represented at Barry it was notable that one of the 8Fs that arrived this year (No. 48518) was built by the LNER for the LMSR.

Among the several 0-6-0 pannier tanks to arrive in 1965 was No. 9629, a member of the 5700 class. In 1986 this locomotive took a place of honour in nearby Cardiff as a static exhibit outside the Holiday Inn.
(P. D. Nicholson)

Another type to appear at Barry in some quantity in 1965 was the Bulleid Pacific, the majority of which were destined to survive. A particularly noteworthy specimen was No. 34070 Manston, depicted two years later, this being the last locomotive built by the Southern Railway prior to Nationalisation. Now owned by the Manston Locomotive Preservation Society it is undergoing restoration at Richborough in Kent.
(P. D. Nicholson)

1 9 6 6

36 arrivals:-	4920	6984	6990	7802	7812	7819	7820
	7821	7822	7827	7828	7927	34053	34059
	34101	35005	35011	35022	41313	44901	73082
	75078	76017	80064	80072	80078	80079	80080
	80097	80098	80100	80104	80105	80135	80136
	80150						

0 cut:-

0 departures:-

0 restored:-

The 'Year of the Manor', eight of these well liked machines arrive from Shrewsbury. Also into the yard this year are 13 BR Standard tanks, the ideal machine for many preserved lines.

One of the several Rebuilt 'Merchant Navy' Pacifics arriving at about this time was No. 35005 Canadian Pacific. It was to be the first of no less than ten examples, (representing one third of the class to be secured for preservation eventually) arriving at Steamtown, Carnforth in March 1973. (J. Graham collection)

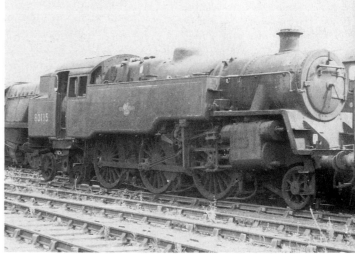

No. 80135 – one of more than a dozen BR Standard 2-6-4Ts added to Woodham's stocks in 1966. This example has since been restored to working order on the North Yorkshire Moors Railway. Photographed on 2nd July 1967. (P D. Nicholson)

Left: A general view of loco-motives at the West Pond site, July 1967.
(P.D. Nicholson)

*Below: GWR 'Castle' class No. 5029 **Nunney Castle,** subsequently restored to working order by the Great Western Society at Didcot, with above, SR S15 class 4-6-0 No. 30828. The latter has returned to its place of origin, Eastleigh Works, Hampshire for restoration. This view shows the engines at Barry in the late sixties.*
(Tony Wakefield)

*Right: SR Maunsell design-
ed S15 class No. 30825
when intact, depicted at
Barry 2nd July 1967. This
was to be the only locomotive
to lose its boiler before it too
left South Wales for preservation. The locomotive is
now at Shipyard Services in
Essex where a new boiler is
to be constructed.
(P.D. Nicholson)*

*Below: All surviving
Southern Moguls spent time
in Woodham's yard. Nearest
the camera is U class No.
31806, now restored on the
Mid-Hants Railway, and
beyond is sister No. 31638
which now awaits attention
on the Bluebell Railway.
(Tony Wakefield)*

Ivatt 2-6-2T No. 41313 in July 1967 – one of two of the type to be rescued from Barry, this one going to Quainton Road, Bucks (Buckinghamshire Railway Centre). Two others, Nos 41248 and 41303 were not so fortunate.
(P.D. Nicholson)

*The only named Standard Class 5 of the Southern Region to survive – No. 73082 **Camelot** at Barry, July 1967 still complete with tender. Subsequently sold to a steelworks, the tender has required replacement during its restoration at Sheffield Park, Bluebell Railway.*
(P.D. Nicholson)

Yet another type that would be extinct today but for Barry – the Riddles Class 2MT 2-6-0 of British Railways, represented here by No. 78022. It is now at Haworth, Keighley & Worth Valley Railway in an advanced stage of restoration. In front of this locomotive is an example of its Ivatt designed predecessor, No. 46521, a Severn Valley Railway resident today.
(P.D. Nicholson)

Right: Beginning to look somewhat neglected, although basically complete, albeit sans tender. U class No. 31625 in the 'cutting up sidings' West Pond site, 24th October 1979. Later acquired for the Mid-Hants Railway.
(P.D. Nicholson)

Below: The London Midland Society's 4F class 0-6-0 No. 44123 at Barry in 1978. First moved to Ropley, M-HR then to its present home at Bitton, Avon.
(John Graham)

Above: Tenderless Rebuilt 'Merchant Navy' No. 35011 **General Steam Navigation** *on 21st May 1981. Subsequently purchased for preservation at Brighton, along with several other Bulleid Pacifics from Barry.*
(P.D. Nicholson)

Below: Churchward 2-8-0 No. 2874 at Barry, July 1985. This was one of no less than five ex Great Western locomotives purchased privately by Mr Terry Rippingale. These were all destined to be housed at the Big Pit Museum, Blaenavon, an appropriate home for these predominantly South Wales engines.
(P.D. Nicholson)

Left: Time takes its toll. The decaying remains of GWR Large Prairie tank No. 5199, July 1985. Detailed examination revealed that in fact its condition was far better than popularly supposed and it was acquired, and moved to Toddington, Glos-Warks Railway.
(P.D. Nicholson)

Below: Small Prairie No. 5553 with a heartfelt inscription. This locomotive is destined to achieve the longest stay of any at Barry, and is to be rewarded with permanent preservation by the local council in Barry.
(P.D. Nicholson)

Above: Speaking for all at Barry – "Please don't let me die". LMSR 8F class 2-8-0 No. 48305 now safely in the care of the Great Central Railway, Loughborough. (P.D. Nicholson)

Below: No. 76077 a BR Standard Class 4, 2-6-0 for which there were numerous schemes and proposals over the years. Eventually purchased privately and moved to Toddington, Glos., arriving there in May 1987. (P.D. Nicholson)

Above: A very useful type, well represented on steam railways today is the BR Standard Class 4MT, 2-6-4T. No. 80097 stands in isolation at the main West Pond site. Now awaiting restoration at Bury, for the East Lancashire Railway.
(Tony Wakefield)

Above and Right: 16th July 1980 and 9F class 2-10-0 No. 92085 meets its end. This was to be the penultimate locomotive to be cut up at Barry, followed within a few days by Prairie tank No. 4156. These two views show the 9F being dismembered, and as left during the lunch break.
(P.D. Nicholson)

Scenes from Sixty Six These views come from a visit to the yard on 2nd September 1966. (P. D. Nicholson)

Above: No. 4247 a Churchward 4200 class 2-8-0T which is now on the Cholsey & Wallingford Railway.

Top right: No. 5967 Bickmarsh Hall, one of five GWR locomotives later purchased by Mr. T. Rippingale. In early 1987 they were all still at Barry whilst efforts were being made to locate appropriate homes for them. To the right is No. 3822 now at Didcot and fully restored.

Above right: 2-8-2T No. 7202, which is now safely at the Great Western Society's Didcot Railway Centre, stands face to face with No. 6960 Raveningham Hall one of the mainstays of the Severn Valley Railway today.

Right: No. 9466 the only 9400 class 0-6-0PT to escape the torch at Barry. Now owned and restored by Mr. D. Howells, it is based at the Buckinghamshire Railway Centre, Quainton.

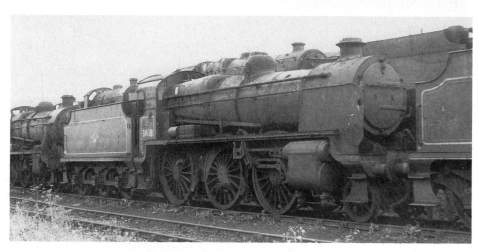

'Battle of Britain' class Bulleid Pacific No. 34072 257 Squadron currently stored at Blunsdon on the Swindon & Cricklade Railway.

Above right: No. 53809, Somerset & Dorset 7F class 2-8-0 later rescued and restored as No. 13809 and now based at the Midland Railway Centre, Butterley.

No. 31638 a Maunsell 'U' class 2-6-0, which had a number of its driving wheel spokes cut through by BR on condemnation. It is now in store at Sheffield Park on the Bluebell Railway. To the left is No. 31806 a well known Mid-Hants Railway locomotive.

1 9 6 7

29 arrivals:-	35010	35027	35029	42765	42859	42968	46428
	46447	46512	46521	47279	47298	47324	47357
	47406	47493	71000	73096	73156	75014	75069
	75079	78018	78019	78022	78059	80151	92085
	92134						

0 cut:-

0 departures:-

0 restored:-

Probably the most important locomotive to come to Barry arrives – No. 71000 *Duke of Gloucester*, purported to have been towed to Cashmore's yard at Newport in error, where an enthusiast spotted the mistake and the locomotive was redirected to Barry – and survival! Some significant LMSR 2-6-0s are also taken into stock.

Wagons are still keeping the yard busy, so no locomotives are cut again this year.

Below right: Collett 2-6-0 No. 7325 now in an advanced stage of restoration at Bewdley on the Severn Valley Railway where it has reverted to its former identity of No. 9303.

Above: The most significant engine to appear on the Barry scene this year was No. 71000 Duke of Gloucester the sole example of BR's class 8P 4-6-2. Seen here minus its cylinders in 1969 it represents a formidable restoration task, but one now successfully completed on the Great Central Railway. (P. D. Nicholson)

A Yard with a View These 1967 photographs show the yard as it was on 2nd July. This was the penultimate year of steam locomotive acquisition by Messrs Woodham Bros. (P. D. Nicholson)

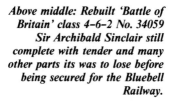

Above middle: Rebuilt 'Battle of Britain' class 4-6-2 No. 34059 Sir Archibald Sinclair still complete with tender and many other parts its was to lose before being secured for the Bluebell Railway.

Sister locomotive, No. 34101 Hartland which became the 92nd departure in July 1978 having been purchased privately.

Above: No. 35010 Blue Star, one of ten Rebuilt 'Merchant Navy' 4–6–2s to seek sanctuary at Barry. All have now been purchased for preservation, with this example, which had suffered the indignity of a smashed cylinder, being moved to North Woolwich, London for restoration.

Above right: 'Merchant Navy' class No. 35022 Holland-America Line, a long time reservation by the Southern Steam Trust/Southern Counties Match Company for the Swanage Railway. This finally came to fruition in March 1986 when it became the 170th departure.

Above middle: Ivatt Class 2MT 2–6–0 No. 46512 on the siding alongside Hood Road, Barry. This has since travelled as far from South Wales as any former resident, now being located at Aviemore on the Strathspey Railway, Scotland.

Ex LMSR 'Jinty' 0–6–0T No. 47279 which has since found a good home on the Keighley & Worth Valley Railway with steaming in 1987 a good possibility.

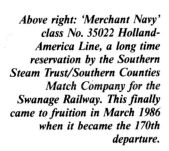

BR Standard Class 5, 4-6-0 No. 73082 Camelot - the only named member of the class to have survived, now appropriately on the Bluebell Railway where it is undergoing restoration by its owners, the Camelot Locomotive Society. Like so many other engines of all types at Barry it was to lose its tender to Duport's Steelworks after this photograph was taken.

Below middle: BR Standard Class 4, 4-6-0 No. 75079 on the Hood Road siding. The purchase of this double chimney locomotive was aided by the Plymouth City Lottery and it is now one of the several ex Barry in-mates to be found at the Plym Valley project.

Below: BR 2-6-0 No. 78018 heads the line up in Hood Road on this sunny July day. Now undergoing restoration in far away Darlington, the town where it was built in 1954.

Below right: The Severn Valley Railway's BR Standard Class 2, 2-6-0 No. 78019.

Above: The Bluebell Railway's sister Class 2, No. 78059 when still fitted with a tender.

Above right: One of Barry's more unfortunate occupants. BR 9F class 2-10-0 No. 92085 that fell prey to the oxy-acetylene torch in July 1980 when a temporary hold-up in the supply of wagons occurred.

'Castle' class No. 7027 Thornbury Castle at Barry, 30th September 1967. Birmingham Railway Museum procured three out of the five Barry 'Castles' with the other two going to the Great Western Society at Didcot. (J. H. Bird)

1 9 6 8

11 arrivals:-	41312	47327	48151	48305	61264	73129	76077
	76079	76080	76084	92212			
0 cut:-							
1 departures:-	43924						
0 restored:-							

The last steam locomotives are withdrawn by BR, so this year's arrivals at Barry will be the last.

1968 witnessed the arrival of the one and only LNER locomotive to reach Barry, No. 61264 which had survived as a stationary boiler at Colwick.

No. 48151 was one of the last locomotives to arrive – this had been subject of a preservation attempt by the Stanier Preservation Society before withdrawal from BR – happily it was subsequently saved in 1975 by a private individual.

Three diesels were also acquired from BR Nos. D600; D601 and D6122 but none of these survive for preservation.

More importantly the Midland 4F Preservation Society purchase No. 43924 from Woodham Bros. and move it by rail on 11th September, via Hereford, to the Keighley & Worth Valley Railway for restoration. This sale and others require BR agreement since their terms of sale stipulate that locomotives are not resold without their permission.

1959–68 have been the years of cutting and accumulation, the next decade is to experience much effort in following the Midland 4F Preservation Society's example in reducing the stock in the yard.

Below middle: Three diesel locomotives were acquired from BR in 1968 but were not to prove popular with either the scrapmen here, or with preservationists. D600 Active was broken up in 1970 while D601 Ark Royal, both A1A–A1A hydraulics, and D6122 a Type 2, Bo-Bo diesel electric, lingered on until 1980. The latter had received a replacement cab, the fading paintwork revealing this to have originated from D6121 when photographed in October 1979. (P. D. Nicholson)

Below: D601 Ark Royal, with D6122 behind, 23rd October 1979. (P. D. Nicholson)

Below right: Among the last steam locomotives received at Barry were four BR Standard Class 4MT 2-6-0s, a type which would otherwise be extinct today. Looking somewhat anonymous in an all-over coat of red oxide is No. 76084. Private restoration is now taking place at South Leverton, near Retford, Notts. (M. J. Allen)

1969-1978
Consolidation

1 9 6 9

0 arrivals:-
0 cut:-
2 departures:-   5322   31618
0 restored:-

Following the example set in 1968, a Great Western Society member purchases a Churchward 2-6-0, a class of which none had been secured for preservation. Eight had arrived at Barry and been cut up in 1959, but luckily two more (including a Collett development) came into the yard in 1965, so Barry begins to fill gaps in the types preserved.

Also rescued in 1969 was the first SR locomotive, again of a class as yet extinct except at Barry, No. 31618 moves to New Hythe early in the year.

These early purchases are of medium size locomotives that will be ideal for the type of operation envisaged by their new owners on the private lines that are springing up around the country.

The last BR locomotive to arrive for scrap was another diesel, No. D8206 in spring 1969, this was cut up within twelve months.

Purchased by the Southern Mogul Preservation Society, No. 31618 was moved by rail from Barry to Kent over the weekend of 18th and 19th January 1969.
The Mogul is seen leaving Gravesend station on the 19th headed by Class 33 diesel electric No. D6584. Note that the steam locomotive was moved with its coupling rods in situ.
(D. Idle)

No. 31618 is seen here on the Sunday morning at Hither Green Motive Power Depot being readied for the last leg of its journey to private sidings at New Hythe.
(D. Idle)

Below: GWR 4300 class 2-6-0 No. 5322 was purchased privately, together with the tender from 'Manor' class No. 7802 and became the third departure from the yard, going to nearby Caerphilly for restoration. This was in March 1969 with a first steaming date of December 1971. Transfer to Didcot took place in September 1973 with the Great Western Society purchasing the locomotive in 1986 from the member who originally financed the rescue. Photographed at Barry on 2nd July 1967.
(P. D. Nicholson)

Barry '69 Photographed 1st July 1969, by P. D. Nicholson:

Below right: No. 4612, 0-6-0 pannier tank, later sold to the Keighley & Worth Valley Railway as a source of spare parts.

Above: Small Prairie No. 5539, five years after arrival but still looking fairly complete. No buyer having been found it is now earmarked for the Wales Railway Centre.

Above right: Rebuilt 'West Country' class 4-6-2 No. 34039 Boscastle, by now minus its tender. The engine was subsequently purchased by Mr. J. Tawse for restoration at Loughborough on the Great Central Railway.

Above middle: LMSR 'Crab' 2-6-0 No. 42765 - one of the many types of locomotive that would be very poorly represented today but for the Barry survivors. Owned by Mr. A. Wilson it is being restored at Ingrow (West) Goods Shed on the KWVR.

Right: No. 47406, LMSR 3F class 0-6-0T - a handy sized locomotive which most surprisingly, lingered at Barry until as recently as June 1983. Following purchase by the Rowsley Locomotive Trust it was then moved to the Buxton headquarters of the Peak Rail project.

1 9 7 0

Still mainly 'useful' engines being purchased, but this year saw the Great Western Society lay claim to a 'Castle' and the Somerset & Dorset Railway Trust secure a type of locomotive that had been designed specially for use in the difficult working conditions of the S. & D. line, No. 53808. Only eleven were built and the two existing at Barry are the sole surviving examples.

Derby Corporation had decided to support a scheme for a Midland Railway Centre and short-lists twelve locomotives of various types at Barry, almost half of these are eliminated as being "virtually beyond repair" and the final choice from seven LMSR engines is two 3F tanks. At this time Dai Woodham allowed purchasers to make as complete a locomotive as possible by replacing missing parts from other locomotives in the yard, and several visits to Barry are made for this purpose before the engines move to BR Derby Works by

The history making Midland Railway 4F class 0–6–0 No. 43924 – the very first locomotive to have been successfully extricated from the scrapyard at Barry. Departing in September 1968 and entering service on the Keighley & Worth Valley Railway in 1970 – an achievement unlikely to be repeated again today! It is seen here with 'Big Jim', the American S160 class 2–8–0, about to join the 17.30 Keighley – Oxenhope train. (D. Cooper/KWVR)

road. This was the first instance of locomotives being moved from Barry by road transport.

An important milestone is passed when the 4F purchased in 1968 is successfully steamed. The very short time needed would today seem impossible, but this locomotive had only been in the yard three years before it was rescued.

No. 53808 moves out by rail and 'stops over' at Bristol Bath Road Open day before completing its journey to Radstock.

Nos. 4588 and 4983 *Albert Hall* move out on 31st October forming train 8X27 leaving Barry Docks at 04.30 for Gloucester Central, where No. 4983 is left to be towed to Tyseley via Stratford-upon-Avon. No. 4588 continues its journey as train 8X28 from Gloucester Central at 11.30 for Bristol St. Phillips Marsh. On November 2nd train 8X28 leaves Bristol at 01.05 for Totnes with Nos. 4588 and 4555 in tow. Ex BR No. 4555 had been at Bristol Bath Road Open day with No. 53808.

Below: BR built 'Manor' class 4-6-0 No. 7827 Lydham Manor was the 5th departure in June 1970. It is depicted nearly a year before in the previous July, looking impatient to leave and remarkably intact. (P. D. Nicholson)

Above right: No. 47327, LMSR 'Jinty' 0-6-0T arrives at Derby St. Mary's from Barry on 21st July. (J. B. Radford)

Derby Corporation's three Class 3F 0-6-0 tank locomotives acquired in 1970 for the Midland Railway Centre. They are seen at the Derby Works Flower Show and Open Day 1970. Far left is No. 47357 which has since been restored as No. 16440; centre is No. 47327 and nearest the camera, right is No. 47445. The latter was obtained in June from industry. (Courtesy Midland Railway Trust Ltd)

1 9 7 1

0 arrivals:-						
0 cut:-						
6 departures:-	5572	5643	5900	34092	46521	80079
2 restored:-	4588	5322				

No. 4588 was the 11th departure in October 1970 but was the second ex Barry engine to re-enter traffic. Professional restoration was undertaken by BREL Swindon Works during the period May to August 1971. It is seen here that October, on the 2nd, heading the 15.05 Ashburton - Paddington through train. This was the last day of operation on the Ashburton - Buckfastleigh section of the Dart Valley Railway. (D. Idle)

The first of the distinctive Bulleid locomotives is rescued and moved to the Keighley & Worth Valley Railway.

Two more Barry locomotives are steamed, No. 4588's quick return to working condition being due to restoration being carried out by British Rail Engineering Ltd at Swindon.

No. 80079 leaves Barry Docks at 06.30 on 15th May in train 8X91 destined for the Severn Valley Railway.

No. 5572 in train 8X63 departs Barry Docks at 10.15 on 8th August for Taunton towed by a BR 'Hymek' diesel hydraulic locomotive, it is reported to have travelled via the Severn Tunnel.

Churchward 4300 class No. 5322 is put through its paces at Didcot, 3rd August 1975. (G. Scott-Lowe)

1 9 7 2

0 arrivals:–							
1 cut:–	76080						
10 departures:–	5541	6960	7027	30841	34016	45690	46447
	47493	48431	75078				
1 restored:–	7827						

No. 45690 *Leander* is to become one of the most well known of the Barry engines – purchased by Oliver Taylor & Crossley, it is overhauled by BREL at Derby Works. Although changing ownership several times it has continued to haul many trains on BR tracks.

No. 6024 *King Edward I* is purchased in April for £4,260.

Those were the days. Having been collected from Barry in June 1970, No. 7827 Lydham Manor entered service on the Torbay & Dartmouth Railway only two years later. Restoration took place at the Railway's workshops at Paignton. It is seen here leaving Queen's Park station, Paignton with the 4 o'clock train to Kingswear on 10th June 1978. (J. R. Besley/TDR)

Below: Maunsell S15 class 4-6-0 No. 30841 was secured by the Essex Locomotive Society and taken to the Chappel & Wakes Colne base of the Stour Valley Railway Preservation Society, where seen 1st April 1973. (P. D. Nicholson)

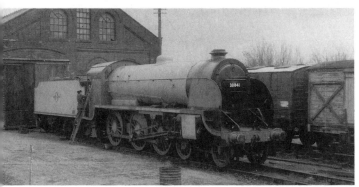

Above right: No. 46447, Class 2MT 2-6-0 was purchased by the Ivatt Locomotive Trust and moved to Quainton Road, Bucks in June. Seen in the departure year at Barry awaiting transportation. Behind is No. 34016 Bodmin which followed to Quainton the next month. (R. C. Hardingham)

No. 48431, first of the six Barry 8F class 2-8-0s to be secured for preservation. This was the 19th departure in May and is seen at Haworth on the Keighley & Worth Valley, 26th August. (P. D. Nicholson)

1 9 7 3

0 arrivals:-							
1 cut:-	3817						
18 departures:-	4141	4930	5043	5164	5239	5619	6024
	7819	34039	35005	42968	46512	73129	75069
	78019	80064	80105	80135			
2 restored:-	45690	47357					

Perhaps Barry's most famous contribution to railway preservation, LMSR 'Jubilee' class 4-6-0 No. 5690 Leander (BR No. 45690). Restored at BREL Derby Works during the period May 1972 to August 1973 it has since worked many hundreds of miles on the main line. After several changes of ownership it is now based at Bridgnorth, Severn Valley Railway. (N. R. Knight)

A dramatic increase in the number of locomotives leaving for restoration, including a 'King'. Over the years different types of locomotives have tended to move out in batches, 1973 is the year of the Standard tank.

Also, a dramatic increase in prices. Value Added Tax is introduced in April, and the prices of steel are decontrolled.

The locomotive moved to Telford thought to be No. 6662 is found to be No. 5619. Identification of the 0-6-2Ts in the yard has always been difficult.

Five locomotives move out together by rail in January, the GWR locomotives (Nos. 4141, 4930, 5164, and 7819) going to Kidderminster whilst No. 73129 continued to Derby. Derby was experiencing steam

again in several aspects, as well as this new arrival, restoration of the two LMSR engines to working order was carried out at Derby works.

Two more classes that would not otherwise survive are rescued. No. 42968 is the only Stanier 2-6-0 and No. 5239 the first GWR 2-8-0T to come out of the yard. The Mogul left the yard on 12th December hauled by BR Class 47 No. 1909 to Cardiff, where No. 37 300 took over to Kidderminster via Lydney and Cheltenham, with the final stage of the journey to Bewdley being under the care of BR Class 25 No. 7640.

Various rescue attempts are under way – No. 7927 is being sought by the Willington Hall Society, No. 2857 by a Severn Valley Group, No. 4150 by a Dean Forest group, a Midlands group wants to raise £3,000 to rescue No. 5224, Hull Locomotive Preservation Group need £3,850 for No. 44123, as well as funds being run for Nos. 30541, 7200, 61264 and 6990. Also reserved is No. 71000 with No. 92134's tender. An attempt to rescue No. D601 *Ark Royal* is being advertised from an Edinburgh address.

No. 47357, LMSR 3F class 0-6-0T was also restored at BREL Derby Works and finished in lined crimson lake livery, taking up former number 16440. First steamed in preservation on 16th June 1973 it is seen here leaving Butterley (Midland Railway Trust) in the company of 4F class 0-6-0 No. 4027 of the National Collection on 29th August 1981. (Tom Heavyside)

1973

No. 42968 is the sole surviving Stanier Class 5MT 2-6-0. A valuable addition to the ranks of preserved locomotives, it was purchased by the Stanier Mogul Fund and moved to the SVR in December. Appearing to be in a remarkably complete state at Barry in 1972. (R. C. Hardingham)

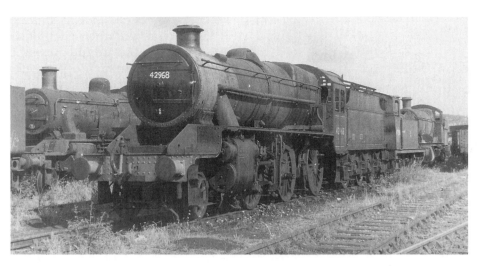

Below: Prairie tank No. 4141, which has come to be known as 'the Hampton Loade engine' because of its long time stay at that station on the Severn Valley Railway. This privately owned locomotive was put up

for sale in a dismantled state in early 1987, but the volunteer gang of workers were hoping to secure it for the line. Depicted at Barry prior to its departure by rail in January 1973. (Tony Wakefield)

Above right: No. 73129, BR Standard class 5MT 4-6-0 is now the only extant example of the class with Caprotti valve gear. The 32nd Barry departure, it is seen at the Midland Railway Centre, Butterley in July 1978, where it is currently undergoing restoration. (M. Tye)

No. 80064, one of three BR Standard tanks to be pulled out in 1973, arriving at Buckfastleigh on the Dart Valley Railway in February. The dismantling work had reached this stage by 2nd June. (P. D. Nicholson)

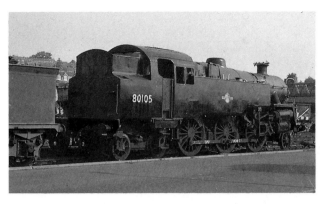

BR Standard tank No. 80105 travelled the farthest of the three that year, making the journey to the Falkirk base of the Scottish Railway Preservation Society. Seen at Barry ready for departure. (R. C. Hardingham)

This was not a good year for GWR 2-8-0 No. 3817. All was not lost however as the smokebox and a pair of driving wheels have survived and are now mounted, like sculptures along the Potteries Greenway footpath. This is made up from the railway route between Kidsgrove and Etruria, Stoke-on-Trent. (P. D. Nicholson)

1 9 7 4

0 arrivals:–						
0 cut:–						
19 departures:–	3738	4144	4150	4160	4942	5080	5637
	6619	7202	7812	30541	31874	35029	41312
	45379	47298	71000	76017	76079		
3 restored:–	30841	46521	48431				

The sole BR Std 8P is purchased for £4,950 – originally destined for official preservation, it arrived at Barry devoid of cylinders and many parts. It was to tax the determination of its owners, but is duly restored to 'better than new' condition by the mid '80s. This year saw several large Prairies move out, as well as the only surviving SR N class.

No. 35029 *Ellerman Lines* is moved by road to Market Overton to be sectioned for display in the National Railway Museum at York, together with one of the few Bulleid tenders in the yard.

Four locomotives are moved to Didcot by rail in April, Nos. 3738, 4144, 4942 and 7202 in train 9Z35 hauled by BR diesel No. 47 080.

In May No. 7812 *Erlestoke Manor* and No. 4150 move from Barry to Parkend. The 'Manor' continues its rail journey to Ashchurch after the Dean Forest RPS Open day.

Tyseley has raised a loan to buy Nos. 5029, 5043 and 5080 to be dismantled for spares for Nos. 7027 and 7029.

No. 5637 is reported to have been moved to the Dart Valley Railway, in fact it moves to Tyseley, with Nos. 4160 and 5080 *Defiant*, after receiving attention from BR staff at Gloucester who rectified a hot axlebox which had developed whilst being towed from Barry.

The Urie S15 Preservation Group (involved in securing two Urie S15s) published the first edition of the 'Barry List' showing details of locomotives still at, or removed from, Barry as at October 1973, price 5p+SAE.

The Association of Railway Preservation Societies advises its members that purchases of locomotives or spare parts should be

The first steam testing of S15 No. 30841 took place on 2nd March and a few main line workings were undertaken, albeit with some mechanical problems being encountered. Following a later spell on the Nene Valley Railway as No. 841, it then moved again to the North Yorkshire Moors Railway on 9th December 1978. Photographed on the 10.50 Grosmont – Pickering train at Ellerbeck, 15th April 1979. The name Greene King, since dropped following overhaul and change of livery to SR black, was bestowed in recognition of sponsorship received from the brewers of that name. (D. Idle)

Below: No. 46521, Ivatt Class 2MT 2-6-0 went into traffic on the Severn Valley Railway in 1974. Seen here on 21st September working the 16.30 Bridgnorth – Bewdley service, waiting at the Bewdley Inner Home signal. (D. Idle)

Above: LMSR 'Black 8' No. 8431 (BR No. 48431) first steamed in preservation towards the end of 1974, entering traffic on the Keighley & Worth Valley Railway a year later. It is seen here on 31st May 1985, well away from its usual haunts, being a participant in the Great Western Society's GWR 150 celebrations at Didcot. This was an appropriate locomotive to be present as it owes its origins to the GWR, having been built at Swindon Works in 1944. Note the painted out smokebox door numberplate.
(P. D. Nicholson)

Above right: No. 4144, 2–6–2T became the 50th departure when it left Barry by rail in April together with Nos. 3738, 4942 and 7202, all being destined for the GWS's headquarters at Didcot, where seen 22nd June 1975.
(G. Scott-Lowe)

Right: No. 4160 was the third 5101 class 2–6–2T to leave Barry in 1974, going to Tyseley. It was sold from there and moved to Plymouth for the Plym Valley Railway project in May 1981, and is shown shortly after arrival in Devon.
(M. Roe)

concluded by the end of 1974 because disposal of those locomotives remaining is imminent.

Rescue attempts continue – No. 4110 is sought for the Severn Valley Railway, No. 9681 for a Hull group, Willington Hall Society decide to switch to No. 4920 *Dumbleton Hall* which is considered to be in better condition, and the Flint & Deeside Railway appeal for £4,000 to buy No. 5668.

No. 7812 is stated to have cost £4,000, No. 34092 £3,850, No. 7812 £4,950 and No. 30541 is anticipated to need £3,000.

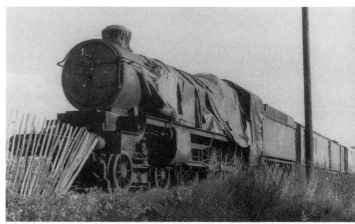

GWR Collett 4900 class 4-6-0 No. 4942 Maindy Hall was purchased in March 1973 by the Great Western Society and moved to Didcot in April 1974. The locomotive was acquired for an ambitious project to rebuild it into a Churchward 2900 'Saint' class. Estimated to require £150,000, an appeal was launched, but without success. The engine therefore now resides at Didcot awaiting a decision on its future, as depicted in May 1985. (The conversion work entailed was fully described in the July 1982 issue of 'Railway World'). (P. D. Nicholson)

Top right: Another GWR 4-6-0 also left Barry in 1974 with an uncertain future, 'Castle' class No. 5080 Defiant. Primarily acquired as a source of spare parts it is shown partly sheeted over at the end of the sidings at Tyseley in October 1980. A change of policy has resulted in this locomotive being restored to main line standards. (P. D. Nicholson)

Above middle: GWR 0-6-2T No. 5637 was another Tyseley arrival in 1974, but subsequently sold to Thamesdown Borough Council in March 1981 for the Swindon & Cricklade Railway. Photographed at Tyseley on 29th May 1977. (P. D. Nicholson)

Right: No. 7812 Erlestoke Manor during a brief spell at the former Dowty Railway Preservation Society site at Ashchurch, Glos., where it

arrived by rail from Barry in May. It broke the journey to appear at the Dean Forest Railway's Open Day at Parkend on 19th May. Photographed at Ashchurch on 15th July, it moved to the Severn Valley Railway on 23rd April 1976. (P. D. Nicholson)

Right: The only surviving Maunsell 'Q' class 0-6-0, No. 30541. Initial restoration work was undertaken at the Dowty RPS, Ashchurch site where it was seen on 15th July having arrived there in May. It was subsequently moved to the Bluebell Railway where restoration has been completed. (P. D. Nicholson)

Above: One of many locomotives which has had to undergo open air restoration is LMSR Class 5, 4-6-0 No. 45379. It was the 55th departure in May 1974 and it was to be more than seven years before another 'Black 5' was to be rescued. Photographed at Bitton station 5th December 1977 before being dismantled for restoration. (P. D. Nicholson)

BR built, Ivatt 2-6-2T No. 41312 was one of only very few engines purchased for retention in South Wales, prior to the Wales Railway Centre project. Seen basking in the sun at the Caerphilly Railway Society on 8th October 1974, a couple of months after arrival. (G. Scott-Lowe)

1974

No. 76079, the second BR Standard Class 4MT 2-6-0 to leave Barry in 1974, these being the first of the type in preservation. Seen safely housed at Steamport, Southport on 30th July 1978. Restoration has since been progressed in Liverpool.
(P. D. Nicholson)

Rebuilt 'Merchant Navy' No. 35029 Ellerman Lines was bought back from Woodham's for the National Collection. Its journey to the National Railway Museum at York was "broken" by calling at Market Overton, Leics, then the base of Flying Scotsman Enterprises. Whilst there it was restored as a static exhibit, including the sectionalising of one side. The very hard physical work entailed is apparently something that will never be forgotten by those who undertook it!
(Tom Heavyside)

1 9 7 5

0 arrivals:-						
0 cut:-						
14 departures:-	2857	4561	5521	5542	6990	7325	7822
	9466	9681	41313	48151	53809	78022	80151
3 restored:-	4566	5541	6960			

Another good year for departures, No. 9466 is an important rescue, as is the second (and last) S. & D. 7F which moves to Kirk Smeaton for restoration.

This is very much the year of the small Prairie, with two brought back to working order as well as three purchased by the West Somerset Railway and moved to their line at an overall cost of £14,000.

Nos. 2857 and 7325 are hauled to Bewdley by BR diesel No. 25 154.

In February No. 9681 is purchased for £3,600 with the aid of a loan, this locomotive had steamed into the yard in 1965 – but made its way out to the Dean Forest Railway by road in October.

Woodham's state that they do not expect any further locomotives to be sold after next April when cutting is likely to start – this work will be spread over the next three years.

In spite of the apparently limited time available further rescues

A further 'Small Prairie' entered traffic in 1975, this being one of the original 4500 class with 1,000 gallon water capacity (straight topped tanks). This was No. 4566 on the Severn Valley Railway where it has proved to be a popular and useful addition to stock. Here departing Bridgnorth, 1st September 1979. (P. D. Nicholson)

are attempted. SVR 2857 Society seek a 42xx, a Bolton group try for No. 92212, a Mid-Hants Railway group are on the way for No. 48518, and a Welsh based advertisement seeks No. 2885 for Quainton Road.

Above: Class 4575 2-6-2T No. 5541, with sloping topped tanks, giving a total of 1,300 gallons water capacity. Restoration was completed in 1975 and it has been the mainstay of services operated by the Dean Forest Railway at their Norchard Steam Centre, Glos. Depicted awaiting its next turn of duty with a pair of GWR auto coaches, 31st July 1982. (P. D. Nicholson)

Above right: The departures of 1975 included some of the last of those to go out by rail. GWR 2-6-0 No. 7325 (9303) and 2-8-0 No. 2857 made such a journey to the Severn Valley Railway behind Class 25 diesel No. 25 154. They are seen here on 13th August at Severn Tunnel Junction station. (Courtesy S. Whittaker)

Right: The SVR also witnessed the entry into traffic this year of 'Modified Hall' 6959 class No. 6960 Raveningham Hall. It is shown here at Bewdley, 14th June 1979 prior to working the 14.00 school special to Bridgnorth. Originally finished in Great Western livery, it has since been amended to BR lined

green, although it is the only surviving member of the class built prior to Nationalisation. (P. D. Nicholson)

Right: GWR 2–6–2T No. 4561, one of no less than three of the type to arrive at Bishop's Lydeard on the West Somerset Railway in September. Photographed 28th March 1976 prior to complete dismantling for restoration. (G. Scott-Lowe)

Below: The three Prairies at Bishop's Lydeard, 28th March 1976, front to back No. 5521 (since transferred to the Dean Forest Railway); No. 5542 and No. 4561. (G. Scott-Lowe)

Above: No. 5542 at Bishop's Lydeard on 13th August 1980. (P. D. Nicholson)

Above right: 'Modified Hall' No. 6990 Witherslack Hall at Barry 23rd February 1974 shortly before purchase for eventual use on the Great Central Railway. It arrived at Loughborough in November 1975. (Courtesy GCR)

Right: Safely at Bewdley, SVR, the only extant Collett 2-6-0, No. 7325. Originally No. 9303, it was renumbered 7325 in April 1958 but has now reverted to its former identity during its lengthy restoration. Illustrated at Bewdley on 1st September 1979 before complete dismantling was to take place. (P. D. Nicholson)

The second LMSR 8F class 2-8-0 to be secured was No. 48151, which had been the subject of an unsuccessful preservation bid when still in service on BR. Taken at first to Embsay on the Yorkshire Dales Railway in November 1975 as shown here. It was later transferred to a private site near Wakefield where restoration in earnest has since been undertaken. (J. R. Ellis)

Above: BR Standard tank No. 80151 was a March 1975 departure being the 66th locomotive to be so honoured. Looking very smart at the Stour Valley RPS base, Chappel & Wakes Colne, Essex on 2nd June 1979 having received cosmetic restoration, whilst money was being raised for the full "works". (P. D. Nicholson)

Top right: A 1972 departure (the 22nd) was the now well-known Mid-Hants Railway rebuilt 'West Country' No. 34016 Bodmin. Its early preservation days however were spent at the Quainton (now Buckinghamshire) Railway Centre. Progress up to 1975 can be seen here in this view at Quainton dated 15th March. (P. D. Nicholson)

Highlight of '75 was the 'Rail 150' event held at Shildon, Co. Durham to commemorate the 150th anniversary of the opening of the Stockton & Darlington Railway. Three of the locomotives taking part in the cavalcade were one time Barry residents and are shown performing in front of the admiring crowds on 30th August.

Top middle: No. 6960 Raveningham Hall.

Above right: No. 5690 Leander.

Right: No. 841 Greene King.

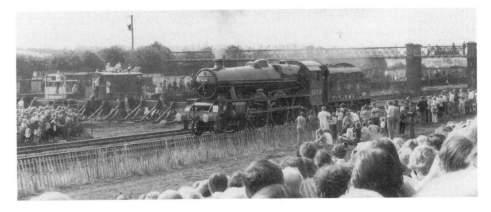

1 9 7 6

The only LNER locomotive to come to Barry, purchased two years ago for £5,750, leaves Barry on 20th July for Loughborough.

The last two engines to be towed from the yard by rail (Nos. 3822 and 5029) are moved to Didcot, all subsequent movements being made by road transport, basically because of the deteriorating condition of the remaining locomotives. Also at Didcot two earlier rescues (Nos. 3738 and 5900) are steamed.

Despite the fears expressed in 1975, cutting has not recommenced. This uncertainty is a problem that is to be with us constantly because the yard can never be sure where their next work will come from.

The Peak Railway Society launch "Operation Salvage" in an effort to purchase eleven locomotives from Barry, the appeal target is £120,000.

Other rescue appeals in 1976 include No. 34105 *Swanage* for the Swanage Railway, No. 44422 for the North Staffs Railway, No. 6989 for Quainton Road, No. 34058 for Bournemouth Steam Centre and No. 80100 for the Bluebell Railway.

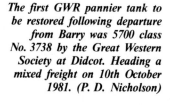

The first GWR pannier tank to be restored following departure from Barry was 5700 class No. 3738 by the Great Western Society at Didcot. Heading a mixed freight on 10th October 1981. (P. D. Nicholson)

Also completed at Didcot in 1976 was the restoration of 'Hall' class No. 5900 Hinderton Hall. Since then it has clocked up many hundreds of miles on the main line. Nicely posed for the camera at Didcot, 31st May 1985. (P. D. Nicholson)

Barry's second departure, No. 31618 was restored to steam in 1976 but it was too heavy for use on the Kent & East Sussex Railway on which it was now based, the work having been finalised at Tenterden. A move the following year to the Bluebell Railway enabled its full potential to be realised. Captured whilst running round a train at Horsted Keynes, 24th June 1979. (P. D. Nicholson)

The MHR's unique 'N' class, No. 31874 entered traffic in 1976, finished in BR lined black livery. Initially carrying the name *Aznar Line*, in recognition of sponsorship received, it was later re-named *Brian Fisk*. The engine is seen here ready for departure from Ropley with the 14.35 Alresford train, 2nd July 1978.
(P. D. Nicholson)

Above middle: The specially cast *Aznar Line* nameplate.
(P. D. Nicholson)

Having just named No. 31874 *Brian Fisk*, Yvonne Fisk is applauded by John Bunch, owner of the locomotive, and Kenneth Bound (right) the editor of 'Mayfair' magazine. Ropley, 15th September 1979.
(MHR)

Above: All shunting of locomotives in the yard has been performed by diesel locomotives on short term hire from British Rail. Here, 08 867 propels Churchward 2-8-0 No. 2807 to the vehicle loading area, 19th June 1981 ready for transport to Toddington, Gloucestershire.
(P.D Nicholson)

Below: Churchward 4200 class 2-8-0T No. 4270 awaits collection in July 1985 having been purchased by Swansea City Council for preservation in South Wales.
(P.D. Nicholson)

Above: Great Western 0-6-0PT No. 9629 is loaded onto road transport at Barry, 21st May 1981. It was destined for Steamtown, Carnforth where restored to static display conditon. It has subsequently returned to South Wales where it can be seen in Cardiff outside the Commonwealth Holiday Inn. (P.D. Nicholson)

Left: The 100th departure from Barry, Large Prairie No. 4110 arriving triumphantly at the Southall, London depot of the GWR Preservation Group. This was on 19th May 1979. (P.D. Nicholson)

Above: No. 7903 **Foremarke Hall** was able to return to its place of building, Swindon Works on 6th June 1981. This was whilst en route from Barry to the Swindon & Cricklade Railway, being perfectly timed for the works open day. (P.D. Nicholson)

Below: A great occasion – 23rd December 1984 as No. 6023 **King Edward II** arrives at Bristol Temple Meads. Note the crane in the background, required to position the locomotive and tender in the old fish dock area where restoration is now taking place. (J. Arkell)

Above: GWR 0-6-0 pannier tank, No. 3738 at Didcot, 31st May 1985. This was the first of the type rescued from Barry to be restored to working order, returning to steam in September 1976. (P.D. Nicholson)

Below: BR built 0-6-0PT No. 9681 storms up the short demonstration line at Norchard, Glos, home of the Dean Forest Railway Preservation Society, June 1985. (P.D. Nicholson)

*Above: It it almost unbelievable that but for Barry, the famous Great Western 4900 'Hall' class 4-6-0s would be extinct today! No. 4930 **Hagley Hall,** based on the Severn Valley Railway is a regular performer on the BR main line and is seen here on 'The Red Dragon' at Kemble, 2nd February 1985 en route to Swindon.*
(P.D. Nicholson)

*Below: The GWR 150 celebrations of 1985 saw a number of main line steam workings by ex Barry locomotives, including those on the regular Gloucester – Swindon – Gloucester service in August. The Severn Valley's 'Manor' class 4-6-0 No. 7819 **Hinton Manor,** newly finished in BR lined black livery has a signal check as it approaches Gloucester on the 14th.*
(P.D. Nicholson)

Above: The first ex Barry locomotive to see operation on the Bluebell Railway, the Maunsell Locomotive Society's "U-boat", 2-6-0 No. 1618 (BR No. 31618), 13th June 1981. (P.D. Nicholson)

Below: A superb example of a Barry restoration – Rebuilt 'West Country' class No. 34016 **Bodmin,** *as seen at Ropley on the Mid-Hants Railway, 16th August 1981. The Rebuilt Bulleid Light Pacific is another type which would not be with us today had it not been for the Barry survivors. (M.J. Beckett)*

Above: Possibly the best known former Barry inmate – ex LMSR 'Jubilee' class 4-6-0 No. 5690 (BR No. 45690) **Leander.** Seen at Steamtown, Carnforth in August 1982. (P.D. Nicholson)

Below: BR Standard Class 4, No. 75069 from the Severn Valley Railway leaves Gloucester for Swindon on its main line debut, 2nd March 1985, with 'The Red Dragon.' (P.D. Nicholson)

Above: Resplendent in lined BR Brunswick green livery, Standard tank No. 80135 makes a fine sight at Grosmont on the North Yorkshire Moors Railway in Spring 1980. (D. Idle)

Below: The last year in which locomotives remained in any quantity at Woodham Bros, Barry was 1987. By the Spring the 28 remaining, were unquestionably in a woebegone state! Two of these last survivors are seen here in March; 'Black 5' No. 44901 and Large Prairie No. 4115. These two, plus eight others, have since been purchased for the Wales Railway Centre in nearby Cardiff – a fitting finalé for the Barry Locomotive Phenomemon. (P.D. Nicholson)

No. 47493, ex LMSR 3F class 0–6–0T as restored at Cranmore, East Somerset Railway. Depicted making its way from Mendip Vale on the up hill climb to Merryfield Lane with a three coach train, 22nd June 1986. (J. Rees)

GWR 2884 class 2–8–0 No. 3822 in the 'departure' sidings at Barry Docks 2nd November 1975, being prepared for its journey to Didcot. Together with No. 5029 Nunney Castle this was to be the last extrication from Woodham's yard to take place by rail. (G. Scott-Lowe)

1976

Looking very smart and complete with cast name and numberplate is the oldest surviving 'Hall' class 4-6-0 No. 4920 Dumbleton Hall. This was one of only a few engines to have been removed from the yard at Barry by means of the western end. No. 4920 made its departure on 4th June 1976. (D. E. Long/DHPS)

Opposite top: No. 34081 92 Squadron was transferred from Barry to the Nene Valley Railway by its owners the Battle of Britain Locomotive Preservation Society in November. Depicted at Barry 8th May 1975. (G. Scott-Lowe)

Opposite bottom: Unfortunately only one former LNER locomotive was to be purchased for Dai's emporium and this came about because of its extended use as a stationary boiler at Colwick, Notts. 'B1' class 4-6-0 No. 61264 was the 'lucky loco' and was to be purchased by the Thompson B1 Locomotive Society. It was moved to Loughborough, GCR, July 1976, being depicted immediately prior to making its journey from Barry. Extensive boiler work has been found to be necessary. (E. Dermont Reynolds/GCR)

Posing as an 0-6-0 No. 4920 Dumbleton Hall shortly after arrival at Buckfastleigh on the Dart Valley Railway, June 1976. (R. W. Penny/DHPS)

1976

Another very complete and tidy looking Standard tank, No. 80078. This view, dated 23rd April 1978 shows it before restoration had commenced at Swanage, Dorset, where it arrived in September 1976. (R. Panting/SST Publicity)

1 9 7 7

0 arrivals:-

0 cut:-

1 departures:-   44422

3 restored:-   7819   75078   80079

No. 7819 Hinton Manor entered traffic on the Severn Valley Railway in late summer 1977. It has been a regular performer ever since as well as making several forays on the main line. Shown bringing in ecs for the 12.10pm Bridgnorth - Bewdley service, 26th March 1978. Initially finished in GWR green livery it reappeared following overhaul in BR lined black in 1985. (D. Idle)

Not since 1968 has there been a year when just one locomotive leaves the yard – and then too it was a 4F!

Three more locomotives are back in working order, including two more at the Severn Valley Railway which makes four ex Barry residents restored at this site.

The Standard Steam Locomotive Preservation Trust is formed to purchase five BR Standard locomotives from Barry.

The LMS Locomotive Trust seek No. 45699 *Galatea* for restoration as No. 5552 *Silver Jubilee* to commemorate Royal Silver Jubilee year.

Another substantial price increase, caused by a change in scrap control regulations, takes place putting several locomotives out of reach of the people about to buy.

The year was to see only one departure from Barry, and like 1968, the only other time that such a low score had been recorded, it was a 4F class 0-6-0. This was No. 44422, acquired for the North Staffordshire Railway at Cheddleton, where seen soon after its off-loading in April (M. Tye)

Standard Class 4MT No. 75078 first steamed on the Keighley & Worth Valley Railway on 6th February 1977. Seen double heading with No. 5820 "Big Jim", the S160 2-8-0, on the 15.40 Oxenhope – Haworth train 19th March 1978. (P. D. Nicholson)

Another Severn Valley success – BR Standard tank No. 80079 at Arley, 7th June 1977. Entry into traffic had taken place on 16th April. (D. Idle)

Above: A very important transfer occurred during 1977 as far as the story of Barry is concerned. This was Southern Mogul No. 31618 which is seen at Uckfield en route from the Kent & East Sussex Railway to the Bluebell Railway, 17th May. It was the first ex Barry engine to be delivered to the Bluebell and it was soon to prove its worth. The wisdom of investing in 'Barry wrecks' was quickly realised and amends made, with no less than nine other engines to follow over the years. (D. Idle)

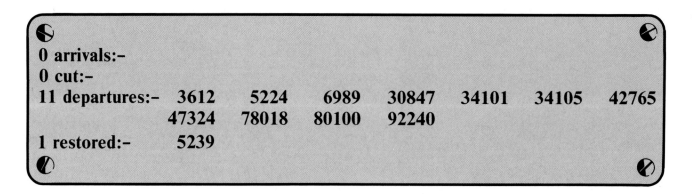

1 9 7 8

0 arrivals:-
0 cut:-
11 departures:- 3612   5224   6989   30847   34101   34105   42765
                 47324   78018   80100   92240
1 restored:-   5239

A better year for rescues. The first Barry 9F moves, along with Nos. 30847 and 80100, to the Bluebell Railway, but No. 3612 is purchased by the Severn Valley Railway for spares.

The first 2-8-0T is restored largely at Newton Abbot works before going into revenue earning service on the Torbay & Dartmouth Railway.

Casual visitors to the yard are restricted whilst loose asbestos lagging is removed from the locomotives.

Concern over the future of the remaining locomotives is expressed in the railway press and discussions take place.

The group seeking No. 48518 for the Mid-Hants Railway has combined with others and moved No. 34105 *Swanage* to their railway.

Groups at Swanage seek to purchase Nos. 31638, 5952, 6695, 42859 and 44123, whilst a match company market matchbox labels depicting locomotives to raise the purchase monies to buy No. 35022 and place it in the care of the Southern Steam Trust at Swanage.

The first GWR 2-8-0T to be steamed in preservation, 5205 class No. 5239 on the Dart Valley/Torbay & Dartmouth Railways, entering traffic on 14th July 1978. The Goliath nameplates were unveiled by Sir Peter Parker, then Chairman of British Railways Board on 26th June 1979. Here, it runs round the train at Kingswear ready to work the 15.15 to Paignton, 17th September 1981.
(P. D. Nicholson)

A less fortunate transfer from Barry was 0-6-0PT No. 3612 purchased for its component parts. The sad remains are depicted at Eardington station, SVR on 1st September 1979. It is understood that the main frames have been further 'dealt with' to ensure no subsequent thoughts are given to its restoration. (P. D. Nicholson)

GWR 2-8-0T No. 5224 was purchased by Roger Hibbert and since restored by him for use on the Great Central Railway. Delivery to Quorn & Woodhouse station yard took place on 25th October 1978. The graffiti stating it had been "Bought by GWS 23/6/75" was of course not correct. (M. Tye)

The year got off to a better start than the previous with No. 6989 Wightwick Hall going to the Quainton Railway Society Ltd in January. (The Bucks Herald)

Maunsell S15 class 4-6-0 No. 30847 was the 95th departure in October 1978 having been purchased by the independent 847 Locomotive Preservation Fund. Loading took place on 9th October. (D. G. Jones)

A home on the Bluebell Railway was negotiated for No. 30847, resulting in the fund merging with the Maunsell Locomotive Society, owners of 'U' class No. 31618 and later 'Q' class No. 30541. The S15 arrives at Sheffield Park on board a 64-wheel trailer of Wrekin Roadways, 12th October, complete with police motor cycle escort.
(P. D. Nicholson)

With air-smoothed casing partly substituted by tarpaulins, 'West Country' class No. 34105 Swanage at Ropley, Mid-Hants Railway on 22nd September 1979. It arrived on the "Watercress Line" in March 1978.
(P. D. Nicholson)

1978

Also arriving at Ropley, MHR in 1978 was LMSR 3F class 0-6-0T No. 47324, being added to stock in February. Seen 2nd July in early stages of restoration when still polluted with asbestos. It has since been deleted from stock, having been transferred by its owners, the London Midland Society, to the Bitton Railway in May 1986.
(P. D. Nicholson)

Above right: An appropriate addition to the Bluebell Railway's stable in 1978 was Standard tank No. 80100 arriving on 11th October. Purchased for the Railway by the Brighton Standard 4 Tank Fund it is regarded as a long term project. Photographed at Sheffield Park a few days after its journey from South Wales.
(P. D. Nicholson)

BR Class 2MT No. 78018 was a further 1978 departure that was later to move on. Arriving at Market Bosworth, Leics. on 31st October, it was hauled to Shackerstone by '04' class diesel No. D2245. Note the driver's bicycle on the running plate! The Mogul was transferred to Darlington in July 1981 for restoration by its new owners, the Darlington Railway Preservation Society.
(M. Tye)

Above: Perhaps less appropriate, but nevertheless a fine acquisition for the Bluebell, and one sure to be a great attraction in times to come, 9F class 2–10–0 No. 92240. Seen turning in the yard at Sheffield Park upon arrival, 6th October. (The two stowaways in the cab had not travelled all the way from Barry!).
(P. D. Nicholson)

Two in view. 'Q' class No. 30541, previously based at Ashchurch, Glos. (Dowty RPS), was transferred to the Bluebell on 6th October. It is seen here having linked up with No. 92240 en route from Barry, making a most unusual spectacle. However, it must be noted that not every motorist wishing to pass through Cuckfield, where they are approaching, was fully appreciative of this that day!
(P. D. Nicholson)

1978

Meanwhile, back at Barry – 16th & 17th December 1978. (P. D. Nicholson):

Despite there having been 98 departures by this time, the main yard was still overflowing with engines, there being three lengthy rows in what was obstensibly the cutting up area. The view from the west across 'acres' of 'domestic scrap' – old 'fridges and the like, shows, right to left: Nos. 5193, 2807, 3803, 35025, 73096, 92207, 7903, 92134, 4247, 3802 and 30830.

Above: Another line in the cutting up yard was headed by 47279, with behind Nos. 4277, 73156, 35009, 45699, 5526 and 3845.

Above right: The western end of the main yard had facing into the sun, left to right: Nos. 44901, 48173 and 76084.

2873 shares a tender with 5972.

Above: 3802 snuggles up to 4247. (3802 went to Plym Valley Railway 17th September 1984).

Above right: 3845 collects rust and dust.

4248 amidst the junk. (Sold to Mr. C. Curtis and moved to Shipyard Services, Brightlingsea, Essex, 9th May 1986).

4979 Wootton Hall maybe in the departure yard but it is in for a disappointment. Later sold back to Woodham's but was to go to the Fleetwood Locomotive Centre with new owners on 23rd October 1986.

1978

5193 during its last winter at Barry, moving to Steamport, Southport the following August.

Above right: 5199 had to wait until July 1985 before its turn came, then going to Toddington on the Gloucestershire Warwickshire Railway.

5972 Olton Hall with most removable items gone. The remains were purchased privately and taken to Procor Ltd, near Wakefield in May 1981 and it is now being restored.

6695 with all its graffiti accurate – it was sold to the Great Western Steam Preservation Group on 28th September 1978 and it did go to the Swanage Railway in May 1979.

7200 a fine and worthy preservation subject but had to wait until September 1981, when it went to Quainton (now Buckinghamshire) Railway Centre.

Below: 34046 Braunton another engine with a long wait ahead of it, but destined for the Brighton Locomotive Works project.

Below right: 45491 slightly more intact than some. Taken north to Blackpool in July 1981.

Right: 73096 the last for the Mid-Hants? It left Barry for the "Watercress Line" 8th July 1985.

73156 one of several BR Standard locomotives later to find sanctuary at Bury for eventual use on the East Lancashire Railway.

1979-1987
... Towards Success

1 9 7 9

0 arrivals:-							
0 cut:-							
11 departures:-	4110	5193	6695	7802	7820	34059	46428
	47279	73082	80136	92212			
7 restored:-	2857	4930	5051	5164	7812	34016	47298

Good restoration progress with no less than four more Barry locomotives working on the Severn Valley Railway.

No. 5193 is loaded on to the low-loader by a Sentinel steam tractor for the benefit of television cameras. On arrival at Southport it is off-loaded by a former Barry resident recently returned to steam – No. 47298.

The subject of Barry is raised in the House of Commons.

Dai Woodham warns that breaking of the remaining locomotives is likely to start about the middle of next year.

Examples of current prices are: 51xx, 4F, SR Light Pacific (less tender) or 76xxx (less tender) £7,000, 'Manor' £10,000, 75xxx £11,000,

Churchward designed 2-8-0 No. 2857 first ran under its own power in preservation, on 9th September at Bewdley, Severn Valley Railway. The first passenger train worked was in June 1980 and the following month it was used in the filming of the television series "God's Wonderful Railway". Subsequent to additional restoration work it ventured onto the main line in September 1985, as shown here, passing through Newport station with a period freight train. (P. D. Nicholson)

80xxx £9,000 and 6023 less tender £8,000.

The newly formed Barry Steam Locomotive Action Group seek to secure the future of the remaining locomotives.

The loading of Nos. 73082 and 34059 at Barry on the same day is quite a spectacle!

The levy which became payable to BR following the resale of any locomotives sold for scrap (up to 50% of profit on sale) is waived.

A more lengthy restoration on the SVR was No. 4930 Hagley Hall, but was seen on the main line almost as soon as the paint had dried. It has got many hundreds of main line miles under its 'boiler bands'

since its September 1979 debut. A nocturnal scene at Bridgnorth shows the engine on 12th April 1980 around 23.00 hrs. (D. Olsen-Hopper)

Large Prairie No. 5164 was completed towards the end of the year, entering traffic on the SVR Christmas services. Found at Bewdley, 11th October 1980 in immaculate condition. (P. D. Nicholson)

The first of five ex Barry 'Castles' to be completed, by a long margin, has needless to say, proved a great favourite on the main line. The fourth departure back in 1970, No. 5051 Dryslwyn Castle/Earl Bathurst was first steamed at Didcot on 8th December. Some more polish is applied at the Great Western Society depot, 10th October 1981. (P. D. Nicholson)

No. 7812 Erlestoke Manor was first steamed on the Severn Valley Railway 12th May 1979 and formally handed over for use on 1st September. Photographed at Bewdley immediately prior to the ceremony, which was held on Platform 3 (above right). (P. D. Nicholson)

Below: No. 34016 Bodmin was first steamed following acquisition by John Bunch and Richard Heather in August 1979. A formal renaming ceremony took place at Alresford station, MHR on 22nd September. (It enters the station with ecs later the same day). The only example of a rebuilt Bulleid Light Pacific in service in preservation to date it has naturally been a star performer on the line ever since. (P. D. Nicholson)

ERLESTOKE MANOR FUND
"CAMBRIAN COAST EXPRESS"
Saturday, September 1st, 1979

THIRD CLASS

Special Charter Train
Bewdley to Bridgnorth and return

To commemorate the restoration and entry into service of G.W.R. locomotive No. 7812 "Erlestoke Manor" on the Severn Valley Railway.

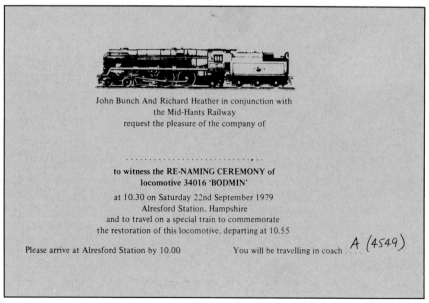

John Bunch And Richard Heather in conjunction with
the Mid-Hants Railway
request the pleasure of the company of

....

to witness the RE-NAMING CEREMONY of
locomotive 34016 'BODMIN'

at 10.30 on Saturday 22nd September 1979
Alresford Station, Hampshire
and to travel on a special train to commemorate
the restoration of this locomotive, departing at 10.55

Please arrive at Alresford Station by 10.00   You will be travelling in coach .... *A (4549)*

Left: Newly restored 'Jinty' No. 47298 is soon put to work at Steamport, Southport to assist with the arrival of the next candidate from Barry, 2-6-2T No. 5193 on 19th August. First steaming of the 3F had taken place on 27th May, less than five years after it had come from the same source. (W. G. Knox/Steamport)

Below left: No. 7820 Dinmore Manor moved even further west on 23rd September, arriving at Bronwydd Arms on the Gwili Railway. Since then the locomotive has been sold and is now under restoration on the West Somerset Railway. (Tom Heavyside)

Above right: No. 7802 Bradley Manor was purchased by the Erlestoke Manor Fund (owners of No. 7812) on 10th August, ostensibly as a source of spare parts for their other engine. Photographed 5th March 1981 when kept well away from public view on the stub end of the Stourport branch. A change of heart has resulted in the locomotive undergoing restoration for eventual use on the SVR. (P. D. Nicholson)

Right: No. 34059 Sir Archibald Sinclair is hauled aboard road transport 24th October for the long journey to the Bluebell Railway. (P. D. Nicholson)

The same day as No. 34059, BR Standard Class 5, No. 73082 Camelot was also pulled out from the yard for despatch to the Bluebell Railway. Motive power was provided by BR diesel electric No. 08 352. (The Standard had to have its bogie removed to fit onto the road vehicle). (P. D. Nicholson)

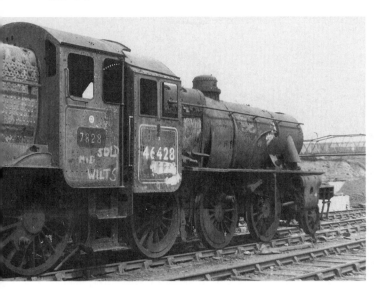

Above: Ivatt Mogul No. 46428 in the departure yard 5th May keeping close company with No. 7828 Odney Manor. This was another locomotive purchased primarily to provide spares, but it was being advertised for sale in early 1987 by the Strathspey Railway, in "Barry condition", and was purchased for the East Lancashire Railway, Bury. (P. D. Nicholson)

Above right: BR class 4MT 2-6-4T No. 80136 arriving at the Cheddleton Railway Museum, Staffordshire on 15th August. (Courtesy NSR)

Above middle: Class 9F No. 92212 owned by The 92212 Holdings Co. Ltd arrived at Loughborough on the Great Central Railway in September. Seen in the early stages of restoration, 3rd May 1980. (P. D. Nicholson)

Prairie tank No. 4150 at Bewdley, SVR, 20th October. (P. D. Nicholson)

Above: 'Castle' class No. 5029 Nunney Castle, Didcot 1st March. (P. D. Nicholson)

Above right: Pannier tank No. 9466 at Quainton, 14th July. (P. D. Nicholson)

LMSR class 5MT, 2-6-0 No. 42968 at Bridgnorth, SVR, 14th June. (P. D. Nicholson)

BR Class 4MT, 4-6-0 No. 75069 at Bridgnorth, SVR, 14th June. (P. D. Nicholson)

*Main picture: No shortage of
candidates for preservation on
5th May with right to left:
Nos. 45491, 92085, 4156, 3862,
5972, 2873, 5967, 4248, 2861,
30825 and 31625.*

*Right: No. 47279 looks toward
the BR Barry Island branch as
a dmu rattles across the bridge.*

*Right: No. 2885 in October. In
the foreground are wheel sets
from 'Western' class diesel
hydraulic locomotives which had
been broken up elsewhere.*

*Below: 0-6-2T No. 5668, with
0-6-0PT No. 9629 right, waits
optimistically in the departure
yard on 5th May. This
locomotive was still waiting at
Barry in early 1987.*

LSWR Urie S15 class No. 30499, 24th October.

SR 'U' class No. 31625, tenderless, 5th May.

1979

Bulleid Pacific No. 34007 Wadebridge on 24th October.

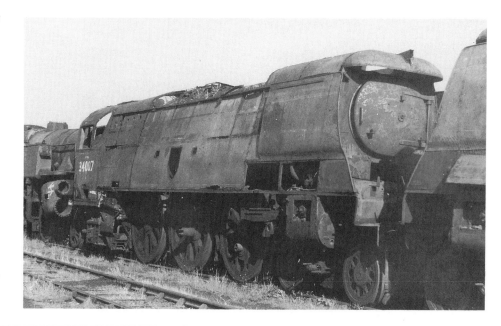

Rebuilt 'Battle of Britain' class No. 34053 Sir Keith Park in May.

Above right: 'Crab' 2-6-0 No. 42859.

The now controversial 'Jubilee' class 4-6-0 No. 45699 Galatea as she was in May 1979.

BR Standard Class 4MT No. 75014.

Sans chimney – No. 80104.

Below: The BBC TV 'Blue Peter' engine No. 80080, 5th May.

Below right: Sister Standard tank No. 80098 the same day.

141

*A surprisingly smart 9F class
2–10–0 No. 92214.*

1 9 8 0

0 arrivals:–

2 cut:–   4156   92085

8 departures:–   31625   31638   34027   35018   45699   80080   92134
               92214

4 restored:–   5619   34092   53809   80135

*A most startling arrival was
No. DS70183, a tender
originating from a C2X class,
LBSCR 0–6–0 – a type long
extinct! Acquired from BR
Selhurst, it was thought that it
might help to sell an otherwise
tenderless locomotive. However
it was purchased for rebuilding
to GWR style to accompany
the replica 4–2–2 No. 3041 The
Queen. Unsuitably matched
with No. 34070 Manston.
(R. C. Hardingham)*

Not a particularly good year if based on the number of locomotives leaving the yard, although the number actually paid for during this twelve months is 18.

In spite of all attempts cutting recommences, the supply of wagons having 'dried up', so parties interested in No. 4156 were advised that it would be cut unless purchased immediately.

In a letter dated 18th July Dai Woodham states "this week we have completed cutting up the first locomotive which was an unreserved 9F – we will be cutting up No. 4156 next week but retaining the spare parts that are marked – we will not be cutting No. 3862 which will be shunted to one side ..." No. 35025 *Brocklebank Line* was next in line after the Prairie, but before this happened the workforce's annual holidays intervened, and on their return more wagons had arrived.

The Urie S15 Group having discovered that No. 30506's boiler requires heavy repairs reach agreement with Woodham's to buy No. 30825's boiler as a replacement for £2,750.

Other prices ruling are 57xx £5,750, 'Hall' £9,000, 4F £7,250, 'Crab' £7,750, MN £7,000 (no tender), 'Black 5' £9,500 and 75xxx £9,500.

The remains of North British diesel electric No. D6122 at Barry on 15th June. To the right in the background can be seen the outline of a 9F cab – No. 92085 ... (R. J. Muncey)

Mention must be made of Frank Beaumont's 7F steaming, this left the yard in 1975 and moved to the old station site at Kirk Smeaton where Frank, a retired farmer, and a small group have restored this S. & D. machine to be seen by thousands at the Rainhill celebrations along with four other ex Barry engines,

Nos. 5051, 45690, 47324 and 80079.

Two individuals, Ken Ryder and Terry Rippingale, are in contact with BSLAG, a significant event in that it is to result in the purchase of nine GWR locomotives.

No. 34027 "made" the daily newspapers when Bert Hitchen bought the locomotive as a birthday present for his wife Elizabeth! This locomotive left Barry in March, returned, was off-loaded, then loaded again before departing for the North Yorkshire Moors Railway, due to problems with the road vehicle.

No. 45690, *Leander,* a former Barry inmate rescues failed BR diesel No. 40 179 and its train near Garsdale leaving its own passenger train temporarily at Kirkby Stephen.

The remaining diesels, Nos. D601 and D6122, are cut in the middle of the year, and in an effort to alleviate the tender shortage Woodhams purchase an ex LBSCR C2X class tender from BR. This was moved from Selhurst in July.

In reply to a question by Robert Adley in July, the Chancellor of the Duchy of Lancaster states that a working party is to be set up to examine the remaining locomotives.

In December two 9Fs leave the yard within a couple of days, for Buxton and Grosmont. While at the beginning of the year, a Northants based group had appealed for funds to buy No. 92085 whilst the Swindon & Cricklade Railway launch an appeal for No. 75079.

The 9F, No. 92085 was put to the torch and within a few hours was reduced to a pile of scrap. The work in progress on 16th July, just before lunch break.
(P. D. Nicholson)

"Spares" – 2nd November.
(P. D. Nicholson)

Right: The next victim is recorded for posterity by a photographer unknown, later the same month. The locomotive is Prairie No. 4156.
(Courtesy D. L. V. Woodham)

Perhaps one of Barry's lesser known 'phoenix' – No. 5619, GWR 0-6-2T. Purchased by Telford Development Corporation it was taken to Telford Horsehay Steam Trust, Shropshire in May 1973. The first public steaming took place on 6th September 1980. This photograph was taken in 1982 at the Horsehay site.
(John H. Bird)

BR built Bulleid Pacific No. 34092 City of Wells was restored at Haworth on the KWVR, but has seen very extensive main line operation subsequently. Its official, commemorative return to steam special, was run on the KWVR in April 1980. Seen at Keighley with 'Pines Express' headboard. (G. Scott-Lowe)

A remarkably speedy restoration in private hands was No. 13809 (BR No. 53809) the Somerset and Dorset 7F class 2-8-0. The work was completed at the Midland Railway Centre in time for participation in the 'Rocket 150' celebrations of May 1980. Captured at NCB Bold Colliery sidings having just taken part in the cavalcade on the 26th. (P. D. Nicholson)

Purchased privately, No. 31638 the last Southern Mogul at Barry. Acquired for eventual use on the Bluebell Railway it is looked upon as something of a long term project. It is now stored at Sheffield Park, where photographed 2nd August 1980, a couple of days after arrival. (P. D. Nicholson)

Standard tank No. 80135, finished in BR lined green livery is seen "ex works" on the North Yorkshire Moors Railway, 5th April 1980. (John Hunt/NYMHRT)

Above: No. 35018 British India Line which was the first Bulleid Pacific to be rebuilt by BR, back in 1956. Secured for the Mid-Hants Railway in November 1979, it was moved to Alresford in March 1980 and was seen having spent the night in a lay-by at Cheltenham on the 13th. (P. D. Nicholson)

Above right: Two days after No. 92134 left Barry a second 2-10-0 was on its way. No. 92214 made its exit on 11th December bound for the Peak Railway Society HQ at Buxton. Photographed shortly after arrival in Derbyshire. (M. Tye)

Above middle: Initially, No. 92134 went to the North Yorkshire Moors Railway, taking five days to get there. However, it has subsequently travelled south again, going to Shipyard Service in Essex. 'Hymek' diesel hydraulic No. D7029 shunts the 9F at Goathland on 24th May 1981. (D. Idle)

Right: No. 5051 Drysllwyn Castle, hauling SVR coaches Nos. 829 and 6913 at Rainhill.

No. 5690 Leander, then owned by The Leander Locomotive Ltd.

No. 7298, the Steamport, Southport 'Jinty', since transferred to the Llangollen Railway.

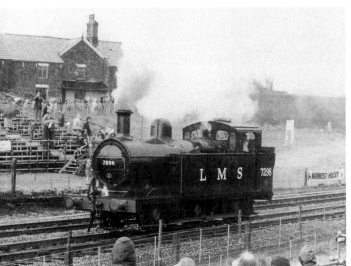

Above right: No. 13809, the Somerset & Dorset 2-8-0 owned by the late Frank Beaumont, making its public debut at that occasion.

Rocket 150

The 150th anniversary of the opening of the Liverpool & Manchester Railway took place at Rainhill on 24th - 26th May. Like the 'Rail 150' (SDR) celebrations five years before, a number of ex Barry engines were able to participate. The five locomotives so honoured are portrayed on the final day of the event.
(P. D. Nicholson)

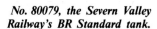

No. 80079, the Severn Valley Railway's BR Standard tank.

1980

The other 7F class 2–8–0 No. 53808. The 9th departure from Barry was scheduled to enter service in 1987 – the 125th anniversary of the Somerset & Dorset Joint Railway. The survival of two of these engines is perhaps one of the most interesting contributions to preservation by the whole Barry saga. Photographed at Washford, West Somerset Railway, 13th August 1980. (P. D. Nicholson)

> **They also serve – seen at Barry 29th April 1980. (P. D. Nicholson)**

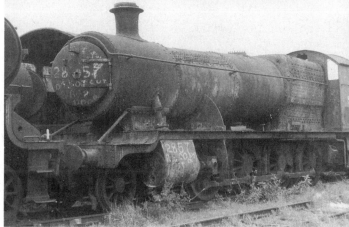

Above: The main yard with right to left: Nos. 34058; 30499; 48518; 80150; 78059; 34073; 34053; 80104; 34007 and 34072.

Above right: Churchward 2800 class No. 2859, later reserved for the Wolverhampton (Low Level) railway project having been the last locomotive to be overhauled at Wolverhampton Works but has been purchased for the Llangollen Railway.

Churchward 2800 No. 2874 purchased privately a few years later.

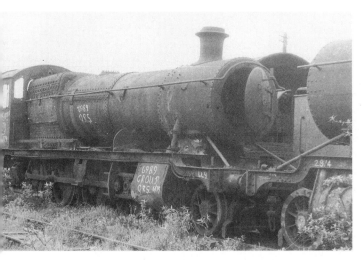

Above: Collett 2884 class No. 3803.

Above right: Large Prairie No. 4121 marshalled with a Bulleid tender.

The doomed 5101 class 2-6-2T No. 4156 - three months later it was no more.

No. 6023 King Edward II Note the rear driving wheels, cut off at the bottom.

*No. 7821 Ditcheat Manor –
before the attention of the
Midlands Action Group.*

*No. 30825 – before the
attention of the Urie S15
Preservation Group.*

*No. 30828, S15 class 4-6-0
which returned to where it was
built the following year, having
been purchased by the
Eastleigh Railway Preservation
Society.*

*No. 30830 destined to be the
last former Southern engine to
find a buyer which was the
Maunsell Locomotive Society
Ltd in 1987.*

No. 44123, the last 0-6-0 tender engine at Barry.

No. 45293, a 'ubiquitous' Black 5.

No. 48624, 8F class 2-8-0 in front of No. 4936 Kinlet Hall – both were moved to the Peak Railway project although the 'Hall' was to move south again subsequently.

No. 76077 – the subject of several abortive preservation schemes, eventually purchased privately for the Gloucestershire Warwickshire Railway.

1980

No. 92207 – later to be formally named Morning Star by its purchaser.

Below: A general view of the cutting up area. In the background can just be seen No. 2807, the oldest Barry engine, in a precarious position at this time.

Above right: GWR No. 3814 23rd December, as smartened up by the Midlands Action Group. Eventually purchased privately and moved to the North Yorkshire Moors Railway in July 1986.

Their Turn to Come – Locomotives at Barry. Late '80. (P. D. Nicholson):

Churchward 2-8-0 tank No. 4277 later purchased by Cotswold Steam Preservation Ltd and moved to Toddington, G-WR. It is seen, at Barry in December, backed up to 2-8-0 No. 2807 the first engine to be acquired by CSP Ltd.

No. 4953 Pitchford Hall being prepared for retention in South Wales, 23rd December but when purchased privately it went just over the border to Norchard, Dean Forest Railway in March 1984.

Above right: GWR 2-8-2T No. 7229 also purchased privately and later moved to the Plym Valley Railway project, Devon. Its extended bunker is most prominent in this rear end view, having been converted from a 2-8-0T (No. 5264) by the GWR in 1935.

Rebuilt 'West Country' class No. 34028 Eddystone at Barry on 2nd November.

No. 34067 Tangmere, photographed 18th October, awaiting transfer to the Mid-Hants Railway.

1981

A record year for departures. If this rate can be maintained the yard will be emptied within three years!

By this time all available Bulleid tenders have been sold and 'West Country/Battle of Britain' and 'Merchant Navy' class locomotives are being bought without tenders.

The subject of Barry is raised in an adjournment debate at Westminster by Robert Adley on 23rd January.

Two men are caught by the police stealing parts and are prosecuted. Another group are caught leaving the yard with Standard locomotive parts as a result of which weekend working parties are stopped.

Several of the departing locomotives have been purchased by what has become known as the 'Group 25' method.

A Redditch group seek initially No. 4277 and then No. 3814; the 48518 Society buy No. 48624 as it is considered in better condition than that which they set themselves up to buy, and a Hertfordshire based advertisement appeals to secure No. 7821. At about the same

A very quick restoration was achieved by the Mid Hants Railway with their U class 2-6-0 No. 31806. Seen piloting No. 34016 Bodmin on a very wet press day, 24th April, two days prior to officially entering traffic. Livery is BR lined black. (P. D. Nicholson)

time as the advertisement appears the locomotive is bought by the existing reservation holder.

A letter from Mr. Woodham states that No. 4979 has been re-purchased and is now available for anyone who is interested.

BR 2-6-4T No. 80064 was restored at Buckfastleigh, DVR but put to work on the Torbay Steam Railway (later known as the Torbay & Dartmouth Railway, and now the Paignton & Dartmouth Steam Railway). It is seen leaving Kingswear on the then TSR with the 15.00 Paignton train, 2nd May 1983. It was little affected by the constant change of railway titles, as it has been moved to the Bluebell Railway. (Tom Heavyside)

Later version GWR 2-8-0 No. 2885 at the Southall, London depot of the GWR Preservation Group on 19th April, where it had arrived from Barry in March. (P. D. Nicholson)

1981

They meet again. Possibly a
unique occurrence took place
on 20th June when No. 2807
en route to the Gloucestershire
Warwickshire Railway and
No. 6634 destined for the East
Somerset Railway were both
parked at the Raglan service
area, Gwent. They had left
Barry on consecutive days, the
2-8-0 having had an over-
night stop. (P. D. Nicholson)

Class 5101 Prairie No. 4121
arriving at Norchard, Dean
Forest Railway Society Ltd.,
8th February.
(P. Skinner/DFRS)

No. 4936 Kinlet Hall at the
Peak Railway's southern base,
Matlock, on 3rd July. Later
transferred to Toddington, Glos
in a dismantled state, but was
asked to move on again in
1987. (P. D. Nicholson)

1981

Acquired for spares. 4575 class 2-6-2T No. 5532 at DFR, Norchard in June 1985.
(P. D. Nicholson)

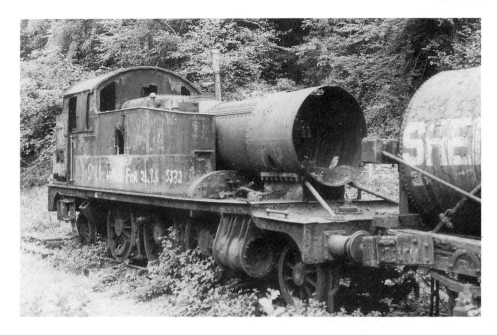

Below: No. 5952 Cogan Hall on arrival at Toddington, Gloucestershire Warwickshire Railway, 16th September.
(P. D. Nicholson)

Above right: GWR Tank Power at Barry 5th February. Left is No. 7200 destined to move to the Quainton Railway Centre, Bucks in September and behind is 2-8-0T No. 4270. To the right is No. 4121 a couple of days prior to departure to Norchard.
(P. D. Nicholson)

No. 7821 Ditcheat Manor soon after arrival at Toddington, Gloucestershire Warwickshire Railway, June 1981.
(P. D. Nicholson)

1981

June was a very busy month for transport contractor Mike Lawrence, as he ran a 'shuttle service' to Toddington, Glos. Locomotives conveyed were Nos. 2807, 7821 and 7828 plus these three GWR 3500 gallon tenders seen arriving on 25th June. (P. D. Nicholson)

Above right: No. 7828 Odney Manor owned by the Great Western Steam Locomotives Group taken initiallly to Toddington but to be moved to Wolverhampton (Low Level). Restoration was scheduled for completion in the summer of 1987, but this view shows it arriving on 27th June 1981. (P. D. Nicholson)

Above middle: 'Dolled up' by the Midlands Action Group, No. 7903 purchased by Foremarke Hall Locomotive Ltd. and moved to the Swindon & Cricklade Railway by Mike Lawrence, also in June. En route the locomotive stopped off for display at the Swindon Works Open day on the 6th. Photographed 18th October 1980. (P. D. Nicholson)

No. 34007 Wadebridge, the oldest surviving 'West Country' class Pacific being received at the Bass-Charrington sidings, Plymouth, in May. It was later transferred to the Plym Valley Railway's Marsh Mills site. (C. Durston/PVR)

Only a couple of months after arrival, the boilers of the Great Western Steam Locomotives Group's two 'Manors' were lifted for restoration. Here the boiler assembly of No. 7821 Ditcheat Manor is raised clear of the frames on 19th August.
(P. D. Nicholson)

1 9 8 2

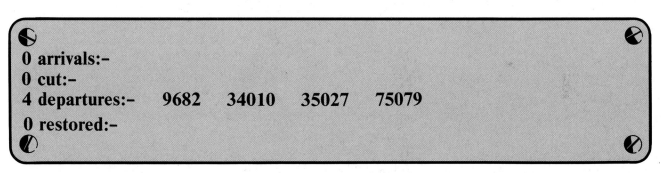

0 arrivals:–
0 cut:–
4 departures:–   9682   34010   35027   75079
0 restored:–

No. 9682 was the last remaining GWR pannier tank at Barry and was saved by the GWR Preservation Group. It was moved to their Southall depot in November but it is seen here receiving a coat of black paint 5th May 1979 in anticipation of its move, when parked in front of No. 4110 which also went to Southall.
(P. D. Nicholson)

1982

Departures do not maintain last year's level and no further engines are brought back to working order.

A notable purchase is No. 6023 *King Edward II* by the Barry Steam Locomotive Action Group.

Carnforth seek two GWR 3,500 gallon tenders to build a replica locomotive for the 'Royalty and Empire' exhibition at Windsor. As there are no tenders of this type spare they agree to use the LBSCR one that arrived a couple of years ago – this can be seen suitably restored at Windsor behind the replica locomotive.

An individual contacts BSLAG as an established railway that he has contacted is not interested in him buying and restoring a locomotive for their line. A site and locomotive are found for him.

A North British industrial diesel arrives in the yard, Mr. Woodham says "I have no idea of the value of the diesel shunter, perhaps someone would like to make us an offer". But the group that had expressed interest did not buy and it was cut up.

A couple of current prices: 'Jinty' £4,250, 78xxx £5,500 (no tender).

Below: No. 34010 Sidmouth marked up at Barry, 21st May 1981. Purchased privately, it headed north to Grosmont on the North Yorkshire Moors Railway in November 1982. (P. D. Nicholson)

Above right: No. 35027 Port Line was purchased by the Port Line Locomotive Project and moved to the Swindon & Cricklade Railway in December. With restoration on target for completion in 1987 this will be one of the speediest undertakings for any Barry locomotive in recent years. Depicted at Barry 29th April 1980. (P. D. Nicholson)

BR Standard 4 No. 75079 at the Marsh Mills site of the Plym Valley Railway project, 6th May – a couple of months after delivery from Barry. (P. D. Nicholson)

Above: This locomotive did not originate from Barry! – but its tender did. The (non working) replica GWR 4-2-2 No. 3041 The Queen which was constructed at Steamtown Carnforth in 1982 for the Royalty & Empire Exhibition at Windor & Eton Central station. Photographed 8th June 1985. The tender was a rebuild of the former LBSCR C2X class example which arrived at Woodham's in 1980. (P. D. Nicholson)

Above right: Among those taking part in the Bluebell's cavalcade on 25th & 26th June was ex Barry 9F No. 92240. The 2-10-0 was hauled dead by Bulleid Pacific Blackmore Vale and is seen here, to the north of Horsted Keynes on the 26th. The tender is notable as it has a completely new top which had been built on a chassis acquired from Briton Ferry Steelworks. (P. D. Nicholson)

Middle: The boiler assembly of No. 35005 Canadian Pacific outside the shed at Steamtown, 31st May. (Tom Heavyside)

Right: Putting in something of a surprise, and brief appearance in Woodham's Barry yard was this industrial diesel locomotive. No. 99, North British 27931 of 1959, 0-6-0 diesel hydraulic, it was acquired from Messrs Roath & Wellfield Coal Co. Ltd, offered for sale but as there were no takers it was scrapped. (J. Graham)

1 9 8 3

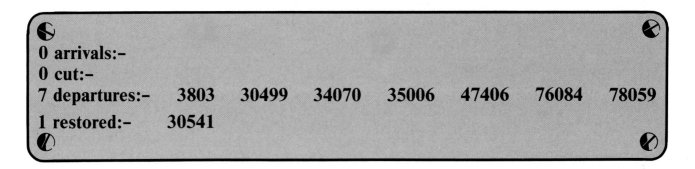

0 arrivals:–

0 cut:–

7 departures:–   3803   30499   34070   35006   47406   76084   78059

1 restored:–   30541

The unique SR Q class 0-6-0 No. 30541 was a very welcome addition to the ranks of operating steam locomotives in 1983. This restoration, by the Maunsell Locomotive Society Ltd in conjunction with the

Mr. Woodham states that following BR's decision to dispose of all condemned wagons at its own works, his source of scrap has come to an end, the wagons he has stored and the cutting of scrap track panels will keep his men busy until the middle of next year, after which the locomotives will be the only work available.

Lord Parry (Wales Tourist Board) discusses with Robert Adley and Dai Woodham, the posssibility of some locomotives, which are unlikely to be sold, going to the 'Big Pit' scheme at Blaenavon.

Bluebell Railway called for the forging of new connecting rods. Restored as No. 541 it departs from Sheffield Park with the 1.35 pm train for Horsted Keynes, 5th April 1986. (P. D. Nicholson)

No. 3803, 2-8-0 left Barry on 13th November bound for Buckfastleigh on the Dart Valley Railway (now the Buckfastleigh & Totnes Steam Railway). Owned by the Dumbleton Hall Preservation Society, a £40,000 appeal was launched in late 1986 in order to undertake its restoration. Seen at Buckfastleigh, May 1985. (P. D. Nicholson)

No. 35006 Peninsular & Oriental S.N. Co. passes the station building at Toddington, G-WR, on its arrival 19th March. Massive strides had been made with the restoration of this rebuilt 'Merchant Navy' by mid 1987. (P. D. Nicholson)

Riddles Mogul No. 78059 was acquired for the Bluebell Railway, arriving at Sheffield Park in May. Photographed in 'as arrived' condition 5th April 1986. Although the Standard 2MT class 2-6-0s were not a Southern Region type, the compatible, but extinct 84xxx series 2-6-2Ts were. As this example lacks a tender the possibility of such a rebuild has not been overlooked. (P. D. Nicholson)

LMSR 3F class 0-6-0T No. 7298 (BR No. 47298) visited Preston Docks for the weekend where photographed on 28th May. On the left are preserved boats, the Manxman and a steam dredger. The 'Jinty' went on to the up and coming Llangollen Railway in Wales a few days later. (Tom Heavyside)

1 9 8 4

0 arrivals:–						
0 cut:–						
10 departures:– 3802	3850	4953	6023	7229	34053	34072
45337	80098	80104				
5 restored:– 5224	6619	9681	75069	76017		

BR's decision to cut wagons 'in-house' lasts for a limited period, but problems cause them to be made available to private scrapyards, even so Dai Woodham warns that cutting of the locomotives is likely by April 1985.

In a dramatic move No. 6023, purchased by BSLAG last year but still at Barry, is resold to Harveys of Bristol and moves to a site at Bristol Temple Meads station for restoration to working order. (See Chapter 4).

Right: GWR Heavy Freight 2-8-0T No. 5224 in unlined BR black livery, owned and restored by Roger Hibbert. Brought back to pristine condition at Loughborough, GCR, it is seen here when visiting Didcot, 31st May 1985. It is coupled to fellow visitor No. 6619 ... (P. D. Nicholson)

Below: No. 6619, GWR 0-6-2T, also finished in unlined BR black livery, had travelled down from the North Yorkshire Moors Railway for the GWR 150th anniversary celebrations held at Didcot. By strange coincidence, both this, and No. 5224 were first steamed in preservation on the same day, 14th October 1984. (P. D. Nicholson)

Above right: Also completed in 1984 and finished in BR unlined black was BR built 0-6-0PT No. 9681 at Norchard on the Dean Forest Railway. Its first day in service was 29th September and was found at work on 9th June 1985. (P. D. Nicholson)

Immaculate in lined Brunswick green is Severn Valley Railway's Class 4MT 4-6-0 No. 75069 at Gloucester, 2nd March 1985 on its main line debut. This was 'The Red Dragon' train which was steam hauled from Newport to Gloucester and Swindon, returning to Gloucester. Restoration of this locomotive was completed in the latter half of 1984 and it was passed for main line running on 6th December. (P. D. Nicholson)

Above: BR Class 4MT No. 76017 entered traffic on the Mid-Hants Railway in 1984. It was the first of four survivors of the class (all ex Barry) to be completed and is shown coming off Ropley shed yard. It has since been named Hermes. (M. J. Beckett)

Above right: Double exposure. Collett 2-8-0 No. 3850 having just arrived at Bishop's Lydeard, West Somerset Railway on 1st March. The wheels alongside the engine are from ex Barry Prairie No. 5542 which is under restoration. (S. J. Edge)

Above middle: No. 34072 257 Squadron at Blunsdon on 26th November 1985 awaiting the restorers' attentions. It was delivered to the Swindon & Cricklade Railway on 14th November 1984, being the second Bulleid Pacific to be purchased by the Port Line Locomotive Project. Both engines are now destined for the Swanage Railway. (P. D. Nicholson)

'Black 5' No. 45337 was purchased 20th March by the 26B Railway Co. Ltd and left Barry on 21st May. It was the first Barry engine to arrive at Bury for the East Lancashire Railway Project, and has since been joined by three others. The photograph was on the occasion of its boiler lift, 9th May 1985. (Oliver Ensor)

Rebuilt 'West Country' 4-6-2 No. 34039 Boscastle during the reassembly stage at Loughborough on the Great Central Railway. Photographed in the Railway's large locomotive shed/workshop in August. (W. R. Squires/GCR)

1 9 8 5

0 arrivals:–							
0 cut:–							
9 departures:–	4247	4270	5199	5526	35010	48305	73096
	80097	92219					
3 restored:–	3822	5572	9466				

After a derailment in the yard No. 80072's trailing truck wheels are cut to enable shunting to continue, this, together with the lack of a cab roof makes this particular locomotive look slightly 'worse for wear'.

By the end of the year there are 20 locomotives purchased awaiting removal from the yard.

Dai Woodham states cutting will start after the August holidays.

1985

2884 class No. 3822 was the first member of the class to be restored to operating condition, making its public debut at Didcot on 28th July. The work was carried out by a group of GWS members known as the 'Heavy Freight Mob'. The livery chosen was GWR wartime black. It is seen near completion in the shed at Didcot, 21st May 1985. (P. D. Nicholson)

Below: Another Great Western Society locomotive was also, appropriately completed this GWR anniversary year. After appearances at Didcot and the BR Open Day at Old Oak Common in 1985 No. 5572 went for an extended stay on the West Somerset Railway in 1986.

A regular performer that season on Britain's longest preserved railway, it is seen at rest in August at Minehead station. (S. J. Edge)

Above right: The only 9400 class 0-6-0PT not in captivity, No. 9466 (the prototype is on display in the Swindon Railway Museum). Restoration was brought to a successful conclusion in time for a guest appearance at Didcot for the 'GWR150' celebrations where depicted 31st May. It was also put through its paces on the Swanage Railway that season. (P. D. Nicholson)

Right: Churchward 2-8-0T No. 4247 is seen arriving at

Wallingford on the morning of 29th April 1985. This unusual view is from the top of a 200ft tower on premises adjacent to the Cholsey & Wallingford Railway site, where restoration is now taking place.
(R. Wickstead)

Right: Large Prairie No. 5199 was taken to Toddington, Glos-Warks Railway by the Great Western Steam Locomotives Group. It was soon dismantled for restoration, this photograph being taken on 27th July, one of the very few days the locomotive was on site and intact.
(P. D. Nicholson)

Above: Small Prairie No. 5526 arrived at Toddington in July and like No. 5199 was soon started on – seen here on the 27th. (P. D. Nicholson)

Above right: No. 80097, BR 2-6-4T at the East Lancs Railway's Bury headquarters on 22nd September, partly sheeted over and fitted, with a non original chimney. Purchased by a group of members within three months of deciding to buy, delivery being effected in May.
(P. D. Nicholson)

Right: BR's penultimate steam locomotive No. 92219 arrived at Peak Rail's Buxton site at the end of May, where photographed on 29th June.
(P. D. Nicholson)

The 2857 Society's 2-8-0 No. 2857 returned to traffic on the Severn Valley Railway on 18th August for the first time since 1980. On 9th September it took 26 goods vehicles from the SVR and made its way overnight down to Newport via Hereford and Worcester. On the following afternoon it hauled these wagons plus six BR five plank wagons, slowly through Newport station as part of BR's Railfreight Spectacular event. It returned later that day travelling via Chepstow and Gloucester. Seen leaving Newport Alexandra Dock Junction yard on the 10th. A unique occurrence in preservation. (G. Scott-Lowe)

1 9 8 6

0 arrivals:-							
0 cut:-							
15 departures:-	3814	4248	4277	4979	5552	6984	30825
	34028	34058	35022	35025	42859	45293	73156
	92207						
2 restored:-	6990	71000					

No. 30825, the S15 from which the boiler was removed in 1980, is sold - the owners aim to produce a new boiler.

No. 4979 *Wootton Hall* is purchased for the second time, but this time it successfully leaves the yard for Fleetwood.

No. 71000 *Duke of Gloucester* is steamed at Loughborough after one of the most difficult restorations accomplished to date. No. 6990, the other restored locomotive is also a Loughborough resident and No. 35025 *Brocklebank Line* moves to the GCR from Barry.

In April the proposed Wales Railway Centre is given until September to confirm their intent to buy ten Barry locomotives and to guarantee to move them by March 1987. Confirmation does not materialise, but their deadline is extended. In October information is forthcoming that the National Heritage Memorial Fund is likely to assist with this purchase, so a new deadline is given, this time it is January 1987.

No. 92207 is purchased by an individual who has spent twelve months working in the Middle East to raise the purchase monies to buy this locomotive, which is then named *Morning Star*.

There are plans put forward to restore a tank engine for static exhibition in Barry town, certainly the town must have benefited from a substantial number of visitors coming to see the locomotives over the last two decades.

Opposite top: 'Modified Hall' No. 6990 Witherslack Hall passed its steam test on 15th July following restoration by the Witherslack Hall Society at Loughborough, GCR. A test run was made to Rothley on 10th August and it appeared in the 'Transpo 86' cavalcade of GCR engines on 6th & 7th October. An appropriate locomotive for this line having worked it previously during the 1948 Locomotive Exchanges. Depicted at Loughborough, 19th October. (D. Wilcock/GCR)

Below right: 5600 class 0-6-2T No. 5643 as cosmetically restored by Steamtown, Carnforth in 1984. Photographed on display in 1986, it has since been purchased by the Lakeside Railway Society for return to working order and used on the Lakeside & Haverthwaite Railway. (John David Bird)

Below: 5700 class 0-6-0PT No. 9629, another static restoration job by Steamtown. Placed on display outside the Holiday Inn, Mill Lane, Cardiff on 1st March 1986. It sports mock up boiler, chimney, dome and safety valve cover, whilst

the original boiler assembly has been kept for more useful purposes. Photographed on 4th November 1986. (Tom Heavyside)

Barry's crowning glory – No. 71000 Duke of Gloucester. The first static steam testing took place on 16th October 1985 and its first outing along the GCR occurred on 25th May 1986, albeit without trailing coupling rods – in comparison with what had been achieved, a minor detail! This magnificent locomotive, a credit to all concerned, is shown running round its train 'The Carillon' at Rothley on 23rd November. The total expenditure of the project amounted to £90,000, and this of course assisted by a great deal of the work being undertaken on a voluntary basis. (G. Wignall/GCR)

1986

Right: A 1931 Foden steam wagon winches up No. 4277, a Churchward 2-8-0T, bound for Toddington, Glos-Warks Railway, where it arrived on 2nd June. Owned by Cotswold Steam Preservation Ltd it has joined their Churchward 2-8-0 No. 2807 which is currently under restoration. 'The Deva' was a BR railtour organised by the Gloucestershire Warwickshire Railway Society many years ago.
(D. J. Andrews)

Below: 'Modified Hall' No. 6984 Owsden Hall is one of a number of locomotives that have been purchased and

taken to private premises for restoration. Acquired by Mr. Trevor Westbury, this locomotive is now "somewhere" in Oxfordshire. (M. J. Allen)

Above right: No. 34058 Sir Frederick Pile was purchased privately and moved to the Bitton Railway, Avon, in early July. Seen here on a sunny Boxing Day 1986.
(P. D. Nicholson)

The remnants of S15 class 4-6-0 No. 30825 - one of the more remarkable purchases and one which augurs well for

the future of steam traction.
(At least there was no need to
have a boiler inspection!)
Acquired for Shipyard Services
of Brightlingsea, Essex to prove
the viability of building a
boiler, firebox and smokebox
assembly anew in the '80s.
Seen at Barry 12th March
1981 following the loss of its
vitals to No. 30506.
(P. D. Nicholson)

Right: No. 35025 Brocklebank
Line was the second rebuilt
Bulleid Pacific to be received by
the Great Central Railway,
arriving in February.
Photographed at Quorn &
Woodhouse, 28th February
1987. (P. D. Nicholson)

Right: 'Black 5' No. 45293,
looking partly 'dealt with' in
the cutting up yard at Barry on
12th December. A visitor to the
yard may have found this an
alarming sight but the
explanation is that the cab had
been removed previously as it
had been planned to convey the
locomotive in parts to the
Preston Park, Brighton site.
However, a change of venue to
North Woolwich enabled a
conventional road journey, in
one piece to be made.
(Lois McGill)

Looking as smart as can be in
the circumstances, Standard 5
No. 73156 was the last of the
class to leave Barry, this being
on the 6th October. Two days
later it was safely at Bury,
East Lancs Railway.
(W. Stevens)

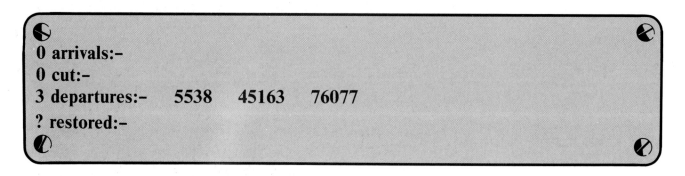

1 9 8 7

0 arrivals:–
0 cut:–
3 departures:–   5538   45163   76077
? restored:–

Wales Railway Centre do not confirm their intended purchase by the agreed deadline which is extended again.

No. 45163's journey to Hull encountered difficulties with the heavy snow that fell in January and was left at a service area on the M6 until conditions improved.

Wolverhampton Council seek No. 2859 for their proposed line from Wolverhampton Low Level station to Bilston – this locomotive was the last overhauled at Stafford Road Works.

A record number of locomotives are at an advanced stage of restoration and are expected to be put into steam for the first time during the year, including: Nos. 5080, 7802, 7822, 7828, 30506, 34027, 34101, 34105, 35027, 47279, 47327, 48151, 53808, 80080 and 92240.

A new steam service on the Cambrian Coast Line during the Summer, to be known as the 'Cardigan Bay Express' is entrusted to a pair of ex Barry locomotives; No. 7819 *Hinton Manor* and No. 75069.

A chance visit to Llangollen on a wet Friday afternoon, 6th March, found No. 7822 Foxcote Manor undergoing its first static steam test.
(P. D. Nicholson)

Above: No. 5538, a much stripped small Prairie at Llangollen, 6th March, where it had arrived from Barry on 1st February. (P. D. Nicholson)

Above right: No. 45163, Class 5MT 4–6–0 snowbound at the Corley motorway service area on 17th January whilst en route to the Hull Dairycoates Depot. This 'Black 5' has been purchased by Mr. Alan Bates of Black Lion Records. (Lois McGill)

Right: No. 4983 Albert Hall was the tenth departure from Barry back in October 1970. Although appearing to be in an advanced stage at Birmingham Railway Museum in February 1987, other locomotives have jumped the queue on several occasions and it still awaits restoration. (John Bird)

Locomotives Still at Barry 1987

12 purchased:–	2859	2874	3855	3862	4253	5668	5967
	30830	34046	34073	35009	35011		
10 reserved:–	2861	4115	5227	5539	6686	7927	
(Wales Railway	44901	48518	80150	92245			
Centre)							
5 reserved:–	2873	3845	5553	48173	80072		
(others)							

1987

The four Bulleid locomotives remaining in the yard (Nos. 34046; 34073; 35009 and 35011) have been paid for by various groups connected with the Brighton Works scheme at Preston Park. This site has no road access, so at least the final part of any movement will have to be made by rail in some shape or form.

Five of the purchased GWR engines (Nos. 2874, 3855, 4253, 5668 and 5967) are privately owned and at the time of writing a site is being negotiated, for them at the Big Pit Museum; Blaenavon.

No. 3862 is being purchased by a small group based at Stonebridge Park.

There are ten locomotives earmarked for the proposed Wales Railway Centre in Cardiff leaving five others which are reserved by various groups or individuals.

> **The last days –**
> *Barry in '87 (P. D. Nicholson)*

Below: Four then unpurchased locomotives representing BR Standard, SR, LMSR and GWR classes. Left to right Nos. 80072, 30830, 48518 and 5553, as seen on 18th February.

Above right: Put aside for the Wales Railway Centre – Churchward 2-8-0 No. 2861.

Still relatively smart and complete, 2884 class Collett 2-8-0 No. 3862 on 18th February. Purchased in April by the LNWR Preservation Society.

178

Above: A much stripped Large Prairie, No. 4115 photographed 2nd April.

Above right: Churchward 2-8-0T No. 4253 awaiting transfer having been purchased by Mr. Terry Rippingale.

Woodham's yard has been used as a film location on many occasions, although Mr. Woodham was not too happy about the time scantily clad 'go-go' dancers brought work in the cutting up area to a standstill. In February 1987 the Royal College of Art was at work with No. 5227 as a backcloth.

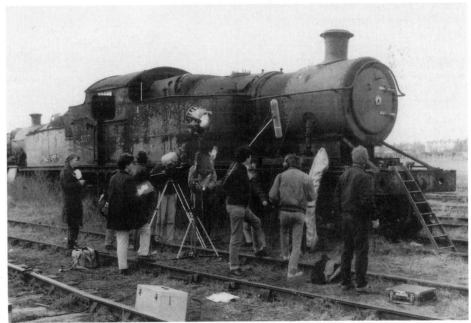

GWR 0-6-2T No. 6686 is another appropriate type for the Wales Railway Centre. This view shows the locomotive at Barry a few years earlier, its positioning in the first half of 1987 making photography virtually impossible. (M. J. Allen)

The WRC's allotted 'Black 5' No. 44901 on a wet April day.

Above right: 8F class 2-8-0 No. 48173, awaiting purchase, the prospective buyers being the London Midland Society, now based on the Bitton Railway.

BR 2-6-4T No. 80072 became derailed during a shunt in May 1985. The result was that both leading wheels on the trailing bogie were burnt off – a most unfortunate occurrence.

A 'sports model' Standard tank, No. 80150, one of the engines to have suffered the ravages of 'enthusiasts'. Reserved for the Wales Railway Centre.

Locomotives Purchased by Woodham Bros.

No.	Class	Type	Built	With-drawn	Into Yard	Cut	Left Yard	Year Rest.	Current site
1367	1366	0-6-0PT	1934	1964	1965	1965	–	–	–
1368	1366	0-6-0PT	1934	1964	1965	1965	–	–	–
2807	2800	2-8-0	1905	1963	1964	–	1981		G-WR Toddington
2857	2800	2-8-0	1918	1963	1963	–	1975	1979	SVR Bridgnorth
2859	2800	2-8-0	1918	1964	1965				Barry
2861	2800	2-8-0	1918	1963	1963				Barry
2873	2800	2-8-0	1918	1964	1965				Barry
2874	2800	2-8-0	1918	1963	1963				Barry
2885	2884	2-8-0	1938	1964	1964	–	1981		GWRPG Southall
3170	3150	2-6-2T	1907	1958	1959	1959	–	–	–
3612	5700	0-6-0PT	1939	1964	1965	–	1978		SVR Eardington
3727	5700	0-6-0PT	1937	1964	1964	1965	–	–	–
3738	5700	0-6-0PT	1937	1965	1965	–	1974	1976	GWS Didcot
3794	5700	0-6-0PT	1938	1964	1965	1965	–	–	–
3802	2884	2-8-0	1938	1965	1965	–	1984		PVR Plymouth
3803	2884	2-8-0	1939	1963	1963	–	1983		BTSR Buckfastleigh
3814	2884	2-8-0	1940	1965	1965	–	1986		NYMR Grosmont
3817	2884	2-8-0	1940	1965	1965	1973	–	–	–
3822	2884	2-8-0	1940	1964	1964	–	1976	1985	GWS Didcot
3845	2884	2-8-0	1942	1964	1964				Barry
3850	2884	2-8-0	1942	1965	1965		1984		WSR Minehead
3855	2884	2-8-0	1942	1965	1965				Barry
3862	2884	2-8-0	1942	1965	1965				Barry
4110	5101	2-6-2T	1936	1965	1965	–	1979		GWRPG Southall
4115	5101	2-6-2T	1936	1965	1965				Barry
4121	5101	2-6-2T	1937	1965	1965	–	1981		DFR Norchard
4141	5101	2-6-2T	1946	1963	1964	–	1973		SVR Hampton Loade
4144	5101	2-6-2T	1946	1965	1965	–	1974		GWS Didcot
4150	5101	2-6-2T	1947	1965	1965	–	1974		SVR Bewdley
4156	5101	2-6-2T	1947	1965	1965	1980	–	–	–
4157	5101	2-6-2T	1947	1965	1965	1965	–	–	–
4160	5101	2-6-2T	1948	1965	1965	–	1974		PVR Plymouth
4164	5101	2-6-2T	1948	1960	1960	1960	–	–	–
4247	4200	2-8-0T	1916	1965	1965	–	1985		CWR Wallingford
4248	4200	2-8-0T	1916	1964	1964	–	1986		Brightlingsea, Essex
4253	4200	2-8-0T	1917	1963	1963				Barry
4270	4200	2-8-0T	1919	1962	1963	–	1985		LSVR Swansea
4277	4200	2-8-0T	1920	1964	1964	–	1986		G-WR Toddington
4550	4500	2-6-2T	1915	1960	1961	1961	–	–	–
4559	4500	2-6-2T	1924	1960	1961	1961	–	–	–
4561	4500	2-6-2T	1924	1962	1962	–	1975		WSR Minehead
4566	4500	2-6-2T	1924	1962	1962	–	1970	1975	SVR Bridgnorth
4588	4575	2-6-2T	1927	1962	1962	–	1970	1971	PDSR Paignton
4594	4575	2-6-2T	1927	1960	1961	1961	–	–	–
4612	5700	0-6-0PT	1942	1965	1965	–	1981		KWVR Haworth
4920	'Hall'	4-6-0	1929	1965	1966	–	1976		BTSR Buckfastleigh
4930	'Hall'	4-6-0	1929	1963	1964	–	1973	1979	SVR Bridgnorth
4936	'Hall'	4-6-0	1929	1964	1964	–	1981		G-WR Toddington
4942	'Hall'	4-6-0	1929	1963	1964	–	1974		GWS Didcot
4953	'Hall'	4-6-0	1929	1963	1964	–	1984		DFR Norchard
4979	'Hall'	4-6-0	1930	1963	1964	–	1986		Fleetwood Loco. Centre
4983	'Hall'	4-6-0	1931	1963	1964	–	1970		BRM Tyseley
5029	'Castle'	4-6-0	1934	1963	1964	–	1976		GWS Didcot
5043	'Castle'	4-6-0	1936	1963	1964	–	1973		BRM Tyseley
5051	'Castle'	4-6-0	1936	1963	1964	–	1970	1979	GWS Didcot
5080	'Castle'	4-6-0	1939	1963	1964	–	1974		BRM Tyseley
5164	5101	2-6-2T	1930	1963	1964	–	1973	1979	SVR Bridgnorth
5182	5101	2-6-2T	1931	1962	1962	1964	–	–	–
5193	5101	2-6-2T	1934	1962	1963	–	1979		Steamport, Southport
5199	5101	2-6-2T	1934	1963	1964	–	1985		G-WR Toddington
5224	5205	2-8-0T	1924	1963	1963	–	1978	1984	GCR Loughborough
5227	5205	2-8-0T	1924	1963	1964				Barry
5239	5205	2-8-0T	1924	1963	1963	–	1973	1978	PDSR Paignton
5312	4300	2-6-0	1917	1958	1959	1959	–	–	–
5322	4300	2-6-0	1917	1964	1965	–	1969	1971	GWS Didcot
5345	4300	2-6-0	1918	1959	1959	1959	–	–	–
5355	4300	2-6-0	1918	1959	1959	1959	–	–	–
5360	4300	2-6-0	1919	1958	1959	1959	–	–	–
5392	4300	2-6-0	1920	1958	1959	1959	–	–	–
5397	4300	2-6-0	1920	1958	1959	1959	–	–	–
5407	5400	0-6-0PT	1932	1960	1960	1961	–	–	–
5417	5400	0-6-0PT	1932	1961	1961	1961	–	–	–
5422	5400	0-6-0PT	1935	1960	1960	1965	–	–	–

No.	Class	Type	Built	Withdrawn	Into Yard	Cut	Left Yard	Year Rest.	Current site
5504	4575	2-6-2T	1927	1960	1960	1961	-	-	-
5510	4575	2-6-2T	1927	1960	1961	1965	-	-	-
5514	4575	2-6-2T	1927	1960	1961	1961	-	-	-
5521	4575	2-6-2T	1927	1962	1962	-	1975		DFR Norchard
5526	4575	2-6-2T	1928	1962	1962	-	1985		G-WR Toddington
5532	4575	2-6-2T	1928	1962	1962	-	1981		DFR Norchard
5538	4575	2-6-2T	1928	1961	1962	-	1987		Llangollen Rly
5539	4575	2-6-2T	1928	1962	1962				Barry
5541	4575	2-6-2T	1928	1962	1962	-	1972	1975	DFR Norchard
5542	4575	2-6-2T	1928	1961	1962	-	1975		WSR Bishop's Lydeard
5546	4575	2-6-2T	1928	1960	1961	1961	-	-	-
5547	4575	2-6-2T	1928	1962	1962	1965	-	-	-
5552	4575	2-6-2T	1928	1960	1961	-	1986		BWR Bodmin
5553	4575	2-6-2T	1928	1961	1962				Barry
5557	4575	2-6-2T	1928	1960	1961	1965	-	-	-
5558	4575	2-6-2T	1928	1960	1961	1965	-	-	-
5572	4575	2-6-2T	1929	1962	1962	-	1971	1985	GWS Didcot
5619	5600	0-6-2T	1925	1964	1964	-	1973	1980	Telford Horsehay, Shropshire
5637	5600	0-6-2T	1925	1964	1964	-	1974		SCR Blunsdon
5643	5600	0-6-2T	1925	1963	1964	-	1971		Steamtown, Carnforth
5651	5600	0-6-2T	1926	1964	1965	1965	-	-	-
5668	5600	0-6-2T	1926	1964	1964				Barry
5669	5600	0-6-2T	1926	1964	1964	1965	-	-	-
5794	5700	0-6-0PT	1930	1959	1961	1965	-	-	-
5900	'Hall'	4-6-0	1931	1963	1964	-	1971	1976	GWS Didcot
5952	'Hall'	4-6-0	1935	1964	1965	-	1981		G-WR Toddington
5967	'Hall'	4-6-0	1937	1964	1964				Barry
5972	'Hall'	4-6-0	1937	1963	1964	-	1981		Wakefield
6023	'King'	4-6-0	1930	1962	1962	-	1984		Bristol T. Meads
6024	'King'	4-6-0	1930	1962	1962	-	1973		Bucks Rly Centre
6115	6100	2-6-2T	1931	1964	1965	1965	-	-	-
6331	4300	2-6-0	1921	1959	1959	1959	-	-	-
6334	4300	2-6-0	1921	1959	1959	1959	-	-	-
6406	6400	0-6-0PT	1932	1960	1960	1961	-	-	-
6619	5600	0-6-2T	1928	1963	1964	-	1974	1984	NYMR Grosmont
6621	5600	0-6-2T	1928	1964	1965	1965	-	-	-
6634	5600	0-6-2T	1928	1964	1964	-	1981		ESR Cranmore
6686	5600	0-6-2T	1928	1964	1964				Barry
6695	5600	0-6-2T	1928	1964	1964	-	1979		Swanage Railway
6696	5600	0-6-2T	1928	1963	1964	1964	-	-	-
6753	5700	0-6-0PT	1947	1961	1961	1961	-	-	-
6960	'Mod. Hall'	4-6-0	1944	1964	1964	-	1972	1975	SVR Bridgnorth
6984	'Mod. Hall'	4-6-0	1948	1965	1966	-	1986		Bicester, Oxon
6989	'Mod. Hall'	4-6-0	1948	1964	1964	-	1978		Bucks Rly Centre
6990	'Mod. Hall'	4-6-0	1948	1965	1966	-	1975	1986	GCR Loughborough
7027	'Castle'	4-6-0	1949	1963	1964	-	1972		BRM Tyseley
7200	7200	2-8-2T	1934	1963	1964	-	1981		Bucks Rly Centre
7202	7200	2-8-2T	1934	1964	1964	-	1974		GWS Didcot
7226	7200	2-8-2T	1935	1964	1964	1965	-	-	-
7229	7200	2-8-2T	1935	1964	1964	-	1984		PVR Plymouth
7325	4300	2-6-0	1932	1964	1965	-	1975		SVR Bewdley
7702	5700	0-6-0PT	1930	1960	1961	1961	-	-	-
7712	5700	0-6-0PT	1930	1960	1960	1961	-	-	-
7719	5700	0-6-0PT	1930	1960	1960	1961	-	-	-
7722	5700	0-6-0PT	1930	1960	1960	1965	-	-	-
7723	5700	0-6-0PT	1930	1960	1960	1965	-	-	-
7725	5700	0-6-0PT	1929	1960	1960	1961	-	-	-
7758	5700	0-6-0PT	1930	1960	1960	1962	-	-	-
7802	'Manor'	4-6-0	1938	1965	1966	-	1979		SVR Bewdley
7812	'Manor'	4-6-0	1939	1965	1966	-	1974	1979	SVR Bridgnorth
7819	'Manor'	4-6-0	1939	1965	1966	-	1973	1977	SVR Bridgnorth
7820	'Manor'	4-6-0	1950	1965	1966	-	1979		WSR Minehead
7821	'Manor'	4-6-0	1950	1965	1966	-	1981		G-WR Toddington
7822	'Manor'	4-6-0	1950	1965	1966	-	1975	1987	Llangollen Rly
7827	'Manor'	4-6-0	1950	1965	1966	-	1970	1972	PDSR Paignton
7828	'Manor'	4-6-0	1950	1965	1966	-	1981	1987	G-WR Toddington
7903	'Mod. Hall'	4-6-0	1949	1964	1964	-	1981		SCR Blunsdon
7927	'Mod. Hall'	4-6-0	1950	1965	1966				Barry
8419	9400	0-6-0PT	1950	1960	1961	1965	-	-	-

No.	Class	Type	Built	With-drawn	Into Yard	Cut	Left Yard	Year Rest.	Current site
8473	9400	0-6-0PT	1951	1961	1961	1961	–	–	–
8475	9400	0-6-0PT	1951	1964	1964	1965	–	–	–
8479	9400	0-6-0PT	1952	1964	1964	1965	–	–	–
8749	5700	0-6-0PT	1931	1964	1964	1965	–	–	–
9436	9400	0-6-0PT	1951	1960	1960	1961	–	–	–
9438	9400	0-6-0PT	1951	1959	1960	1961	–	–	–
9439	9400	0-6-0PT	1951	1959	1960	1961	–	–	–
9443	9400	0-6-0PT	1951	1959	1960	1961	–	–	–
9445	9400	0-6-0PT	1951	1960	1961	1965	–	–	–
9449	9400	0-6-0PT	1951	1960	1961	1965	–	–	–
9459	9400	0-6-0PT	1951	1959	1960	1961	–	–	–
9462	9400	0-6-0PT	1951	1960	1961	1965	–	–	–
9466	9400	0-6-0PT	1952	1964	1965	–	1975	1985	Bucks Rly Centre
9468	9400	0-6-0PT	1952	1960	1961	1965	–	–	–
9491	9400	0-6-0PT	1954	1959	1960	1965	–	–	–
9492	9400	0-6-0PT	1954	1959	1960	1962	–	–	–
9496	9400	0-6-0PT	1954	1959	1960	1961	–	–	–
9499	9400	0-6-0PT	1955	1959	1961	1965	–	–	–
9629	5700	0-6-0PT	1945	1964	1965	–	1981	Static	Cardiff Hotel
9681	5700	0-6-0PT	1949	1965	1965	–	1975	1984	DFR Norchard
9682	5700	0-6-0PT	1949	1965	1965	–	1982		GWRPG Southall
30499	S15	4-6-0	1920	1964	1964	–	1983		MHR Ropley
30506	S15	4-6-0	1920	1964	1964	–	1976		MHR Ropley
30512	S15	4-6-0	1920	1964	1964	1965	–	–	–
30541	Q	0-6-0	1939	1964	1965	–	1974	1983	Bluebell Rly Sheffield Park
30825	S15	4-6-0	1927	1964	1964	–	1986		Brightlingsea, Essex
30828	S15	4-6-0	1927	1964	1964	–	1981		BREL Eastleigh
30830	S15	4-6-0	1927	1964	1964				Barry
30841	S15	4-6-0	1936	1964	1964	–	1972	1974	NYMR Grosmont
30844	S15	4-6-0	1936	1964	1964	1965	–	–	–
30847	S15	4-6-0	1936	1964	1964	–	1978		Bluebell Rly Sheffield Park
31618	U	2-6-0	1928	1964	1964	–	1969	1976	Bluebell Rly Sheffield Park
31625	U	2-6-0	1929	1964	1964	–	1980		MHR Ropley
31638	U	2-6-0	1931	1964	1964	–	1980		Bluebell Rly Sheffield Park
31806	U	2-6-0	1928	1964	1964	–	1976	1981	MHR Ropley
31874	N	2-6-0	1925	1964	1964	–	1974	1976	MHR Ropley
34007	WC	4-6-2	1945	1965	1965	–	1981		PVR Plymouth
34010	WC	4-6-2	1945	1965	1965	–	1982		NYMR Grosmont
34016	WC	4-6-2	1945	1964	1964	–	1972	1979	MHR Ropley
34027	WC	4-6-2	1946	1964	1964	–	1980		SVR Bridgnorth
34028	WC	4-6-2	1946	1964	1964	–	1986		Sellindge, Kent
34039	WC	4-6-2	1946	1965	1965	–	1973		GCR Loughborough
34045	WC	4-6-2	1946	1964	1965	1965	–	–	–
34046	WC	4-6-2	1946	1965	1965				Barry
34053	BB	4-6-2	1947	1965	1966	–	1984		Kingston upon Hull
34058	BB	4-6-2	1947	1964	1964	–	1986		Bitton Railway
34059	BB	4-6-2	1947	1966	1966	–	1979		Bluebell Rly Sheffield Park
34067	BB	4-6-2	1947	1963	1965	–	1981		MHR Ropley
34070	BB	4-6-2	1947	1964	1965	–	1983		Richborough, Kent
34072	BB	4-6-2	1948	1964	1964	–	1984		SCR Blunsdon
34073	BB	4-6-2	1948	1964	1964				Barry
34081	BB	4-6-2	1948	1964	1965	–	1976		NVR Peterborough
34092	WC	4-6-2	1949	1964	1965	–	1971	1980	Steamtown, Carnforth
34094	WC	4-6-2	1949	1964	1964	1965	–	–	–
34101	WC	4-6-2	1950	1966	1966	–	1978		Derby
34105	WC	4-6-2	1950	1964	1965	–	1978		MHR Ropley
35005	MN	4-6-2	1941	1965	1966	–	1973		Steamtown, Carnforth
35006	MN	4-6-2	1941	1964	1965	–	1983		G-WR Toddington
35009	MN	4-6-2	1942	1964	1964				Barry
35010	MN	4-6-2	1942	1966	1967		1985		N. Woolwich
35011	MN	4-6-2	1944	1966	1966				Barry
35018	MN	4-6-2	1945	1964	1964	–	1980		MHR Ropley
35022	MN	4-6-2	1948	1966	1966	–	1986		Swanage Railway
35025	MN	4-6-2	1948	1964	1964	–	1986		GCR Quorn & Woodhouse
35027	MN	4-6-2	1948	1966	1967	–	1982		SCR Blunsdon
35029	MN	4-6-2	1949	1966	1967	1974	Sec-tioned		NRM York
41248	2MT	2-6-2T	1949	1964	1965	1965	–	–	–
41303	2MT	2-6-2T	1952	1964	1965	1965	–	–	–
41312	2MT	2-6-2T	1952	1967	1968	–	1974		Caerphilly
41313	2MT	2-6-2T	1952	1965	1966	–	1975		Bucks Rly Centre
42765	5MT 'Crab'	2-6-0	1927	1966	1967	–	1978		KWVR Ingrow West
42859	5MT 'Crab'	2-6-0	1930	1966	1967	–	1986		Kingston upon Hull

No.	Class	Type	Built	With-drawn	Into Yard	Cut	Left Yard	Year Rest.	Current site
42968	5MT	2-6-0	1934	1966	1967	–	1973		SVR Bridgnorth
43924	4F	0-6-0	1920	1965	1965	–	1968	1970	KWVR Haworth
44123	4F	0-6-0	1925	1965	1965	–	1981		Bitton Railway
44422	4F	0-6-0	1927	1965	1965	–	1977		NSR Cheddleton
44901	5MT	4-6-0	1945	1965	1966				Barry
45163	5MT	4-6-0	1935	1965	1965	–	1987		Kingston upon Hull
45293	5MT	4-6-0	1936	1965	1965	–	1986		N. Woolwich
45337	5MT	4-6-0	1937	1965	1965	–	1984		ELR Bury
45379	5MT	4-6-0	1937	1965	1965	–	1974		Bitton Railway
45491	5MT	4-6-0	1943	1965	1965	–	1981		Fleetwood Loco. Centre
45690	'Jubilee'	4-6-0	1936	1964	1964	–	1972	1973	SVR Bridgnorth
45699	'Jubilee'	4-6-0	1936	1964	1965	–	1980		SVR
46428	2MT	2-6-0	1948	1966	1967	–	1979		ELR Bury
46447	2MT	2-6-0	1950	1966	1967	–	1972		Bucks Rly Centre
46512	2MT	2-6-0	1952	1966	1967	–	1973		Strathspey Rly Aviemore
46521	2MT	2-6-0	1953	1966	1967	–	1971	1974	SVR Bridgnorth
47279	3F	0-6-0T	1924	1966	1967	–	1979		KWVR Haworth
47298	3F	0-6-0T	1924	1966	1967	–	1974	1979	Llangollen Railway
47324	3F	0-6-0T	1926	1966	1967	–	1978		Bitton Railway
47327	3F	0-6-0T	1926	1966	1968	–	1970		MRC Butterley
47357	3F	0-6-0T	1926	1966	1967	–	1970	1973	MRC Butterley
47406	3F	0-6-0T	1926	1966	1967	–	1983		PRS Buxton
47493	3F	0-6-0T	1927	1966	1967	–	1972	1976	ESR Cranmore
48151	8F	2-8-0	1942	1968	1968	–	1975		MRC Butterley
48173	8F	2-8-0	1943	1965	1965				Barry
48305	8F	2-8-0	1943	1968	1968	–	1985		GCR Loughborough
48431	8F	2-8-0	1944	1964	1964	–	1972	1974	KWVR Haworth
48518	8F	2-8-0	1944	1965	1965				Barry
48624	8F	2-8-0	1943	1965	1965	–	1981		PRS Buxton
53808	7F	2-8-0	1925	1964	1964	–	1970		WSR Washford
53809	7F	2-8-0	1925	1964	1964	–	1975	1980	MRC Butterley
61264	B1	4-6-0	1947	1965	1968	–	1976		GCR Loughborough
71000	8P	4-6-2	1954	1962	1967	–	1974	1986	GCR Loughborough
73082	5MT	4-6-0	1955	1966	1966	–	1979		Bluebell Rly Sheffield Park
73096	5MT	4-6-0	1955	1967	1967	–	1985		MHR Ropley
73129	5MT	4-6-0	1956	1967	1968	–	1973		MRC Butterley
73156	5MT	4-6-0	1956	1967	1967	–	1986		ELR Bury
75014	4MT	4-6-0	1951	1966	1967	–	1981		NYMR Grosmont
75069	4MT	4-6-0	1955	1966	1967	–	1973	1984	SVR Bridgnorth
75078	4MT	4-6-0	1956	1966	1966	–	1972	1977	KWVR Haworth
75079	4MT	4-6-0	1956	1966	1967	–	1982		PVR Plymouth
76017	4MT	2-6-0	1953	1965	1966	–	1974	1984	MHR Ropley
76077	4MT	2-6-0	1956	1967	1968	–	1987		G-WR Toddington
76079	4MT	2-6-0	1957	1967	1968	–	1974		Liverpool
76080	4MT	2-6-0	1957	1967	1968	1972	–	–	–
76084	4MT	2-6-0	1957	1967	1968	–	1983		N. Leverton, Notts.
78018	2MT	2-6-0	1954	1966	1967	–	1978		Darlington
78019	2MT	2-6-0	1954	1966	1967	–	1973		SVR Bridgnorth
78022	2MT	2-6-0	1954	1966	1967	–	1975		KWVR Haworth
78059	2MT	2-6-0	1956	1966	1967	–	1983		Bluebell Rly Sheffield Park
80064	4MT	2-6-4T	1953	1965	1966	–	1973	1981	Bluebell Rly Sheffield Park
80067	4MT	2-6-4T	1953	1965	1965	1965	–	–	
80072	4MT	2-6-4T	1953	1965	1966				Barry
80078	4MT	2-6-4T	1954	1965	1966	–	1976		Swanage Railway
80079	4MT	2-6-4T	1954	1965	1966	–	1971	1977	SVR Bridgnorth
80080	4MT	2-6-4T	1954	1965	1966	–	1980		MRC Butterley
80097	4MT	2-6-4T	1954	1965	1966	–	1985		ELR Bury
80098	4MT	2-6-4T	1954	1965	1966	–	1984		MRC Butterley
80100	4MT	2-6-4T	1955	1965	1966	–	1978		Bluebell Rly Sheffield Park
80104	4MT	2-6-4T	1955	1965	1966	–	1984		Swanage Railway
80105	4MT	2-6-4T	1955	1965	1966	–	1973		SRPS Falkirk
80135	4MT	2-6-4T	1956	1965	1966	–	1973	1980	NYMR Grosmont
80136	4MT	2-6-4T	1956	1965	1966	–	1979		NSR Cheddleton
80150	4MT	2-6-4T	1956	1965	1966				Barry
80151	4MT	2-6-4T	1957	1967	1967	–	1975		Stour Valley Rly
92085	9F	2-10-0	1956	1966	1967	1980	–	–	–
92134	9F	2-10-0	1957	1966	1967	–	1980		Brightlingsea, Essex
92207	9F	2-10-0	1959	1964	1964	–	1986		ELR Bury
92212	9F	2-10-0	1959	1968	1968	–	1979		GCR Loughborough
92214	9F	2-10-0	1959	1965	1965	–	1980		PRS Buxton
92219	9F	2-10-0	1960	1965	1965	–	1985		PRS Buxton
92232	9F	2-10-0	1958	1964	1965	1965	–	–	
92240	9F	2-10-0	1958	1965	1965	–	1978		Bluebell Rly Sheffield Park
92245	9F	2-10-0	1958	1964	1965				Barry

Locomotive Departures from Barry.

1	43924	SEPT	1968	Midland 4F Pres. Society	KWVR. Haworth.*
2	31618	JAN	1969	Southern Mogul Pres. Society	New Hythe, Kent.*
3	5322	MAR		Privately	Caerphilly.*
4	5051	FEB	1970	Privately	GWS Didcot.*
5	7827	JUNE		Dart Valley Rly Association	DVR Buckfastleigh.*
6	47327	JULY		Derby Corporation	BREL Derby.
7	47357			Derby Corporation	BREL Derby.
8	4566	AUG		4566 Fund	SVR Bridgnorth.*
9	53808	OCT		S & D Railway Trust	Radstock.*
10	4983			Birmingham Railway Museum	Tyseley.*
11	4588	NOV		Dart Valley Railway	Buckfastleigh.*
12	46521	MAR	1971	Severn Valley Railway	SVR Bridgnorth.*
13	80079	MAY		Passenger Tank Fund	SVR Bridgnorth.*
14	5900	JUNE		Great Western Society	GWS Didcot.*
15	5572	AUG		Great Western Society	Taunton.*
16	5643	SEPT		Eastern Valleys Railway	Cwmbran.
17	34092	OCT		Privately	KWVR Haworth.
18	45690	MAY	1972	Oliver, Taylor & Crossley	BREL Derby.
19	48431			Keighley & Worth Valley Rly	KWVR Haworth.
20	46447	JUNE		Ivatt Locomotive Trust	Quainton Road, Bucks.
21	75078			Std 4 Loco. Pres. Society	KWVR Haworth.
22	34016	JULY		Privately	Quainton Road, Bucks.
23	7027	AUG		Birmingham Railway Museum	Tyseley.
24	30841	SEPT		Essex Locomotive Society	Stour Valley Rly, Chapel & Wakes Colne.
25	5541	OCT		Forest Prairie Fund	DFR Parkend.*
26	6960			Privately	Steamtown, Carnforth.
27	47493	DEC		Privately	Radstock.
28	4141	JAN	1973	Privately	SVR Hampton Loade.*
29	4930			Severn Valley Railway	SVR Bridgnorth.*
30	5164			51xx Fund	SVR Bridgnorth.*
31	7819			Severn Valley Railway	SVR Bridgnorth.*
32	73129			Derby Corporation	BREL Derby.*
33	34039			Privately	GCR Loughborough.
34	80064	FEB		Privately	DVR Buckfastleigh.
35	78019	MAR		Severn Valley Railway	SVR Bridgnorth.
36	6024			King Pres. Society	Quainton Road, Bucks.
37	75069			The 75069 Fund	SVR Bridgnorth.*
38	35005			Privately	Steamtown, Carnforth.
39	80135	APR		Privately	NYMR Grosmont.
40	5619	MAY		Telford Development Corpn.	Telford.
41	46512			Privately	SVR Bridgnorth.*
42	5239	JUNE		Dart Valley Railway	BR Newton Abbot.*
43	5043	SEPT		Birmingham Railway Museum	Tyseley.
44	80105	OCT		Loco. Owners Group	SRPS Falkirk.
45	42968	DEC		Stanier Mogul Pres. Society	SVR Bridgnorth.*
46	76017	JAN	1974	Std 4 Preservation Group	Quainton Road, Bucks.
47	35029			National Railway Museum	Market Overton.
48	31874	MAR		Privately	MHR Alresford.
49	3738	APR		Privately	GWS Didcot.*
50	4144			Privately	GWS Didcot.*
51	4942			Great Western Society	GWS Didcot.*
52	7202			Great Western Society	GWS Didcot.*
53	71000			Duke of Gloucester Steam Loco. Trust	GCR Loughborough.
54	30541	MAY		Southern Q Fund	Dowty RPS Ashchurch.
55	45379			Bristol Black 5 Society	Bitton Railway.
56	7812			Erlestoke Manor Fund	SVR Bewdley.*
57	4150			4150 Loco. Fund	DFR Parkend.*
58	47298			Liverpool Loco. Pres. Group	Steamport, Southport.
59	76079	JULY		Privately	Steamport, Southport.
60	4160	AUG		Birmingham Railway Museum	Tyseley.*
61	5637			Birmingham Railway Museum	Tyseley.*
62	5080			Birmingham Railway Museum	Tyseley.*
63	41312			Privately	Caerphilly.
64	6619	OCT		6619 Fund	NYMR Grosmont.
65	7822	JAN	1975	Foxcote Manor Society	Oswestry.
66	80151	MAR		Anglian Loco. Group	Stour Valley Rly, Chappel & Wakes Colne.

No.	Loco. No.	Month	Year	Purchaser	Moved to (*by rail)
67	78022	JUNE		Std 4 Loco. Pres. Society	KWVR Oakworth.
68	41313	JULY		Ivatt Locomotive Trust	Quainton Road, Bucks.
69	2857	AUG		2857 Fund	SVR Bewdley.*
70	7325			GW (SVR) Association	SVR Bewdley.*
71	4561	SEPT		West Somerset Railway	WSR Bishop's Lydeard.
72	5521			West Somerset Railway	WSR Bishop's Lydeard.
73	5542			West Somerset Railway	WSR Bishop's Lydeard.
74	9466			Privately	Quainton Road, Bucks.
75	9681	OCT		Forest Pannier Fund	DFR Norchard.
76	6990	NOV		Witherslack Hall Society	GCR Loughborough.
77	48151			Privately	YDR Embsay.
78	53809	DEC		Privately	Kirk Smeaton, N. Yorks.
79	30506	APR	1976	Urie S15 Preservation Group	MHR Ropley.
80	3822	MAY		Great Western Society	GWS Didcot.*
81	5029			Great Western Society	GWS Didcot.*
82	4920	JUNE		Dumbleton Hall Pres. Society	DVR Buckfastleigh.
83	61264	JULY		Thompson B1 Locomotive Society	GCR Loughborough.
84	80078	SEPT		Southern Steam Trust	Swanage Railway.
85	31806	OCT		Privately	MHR Ropley.
86	34081	NOV		BofB Locomotive Pres. Society	NVR Wansford.
87	44422	APR	1977	North Staffs. Railway	NSR Cheddleton.
88	6989	JAN	1978	Wightwick Hall Fund, QRS	Quainton Road, Bucks.
89	47324	FEB		Fowler 3F Society	MHR Ropley.
90	34105	MAR		34105 Light Pacific Group	MHR Ropley.
91	42765	APR		Privately	KWVR Ingrow West.
92	34101	JULY		Privately	Derby.
93	92240	OCT		BR Class 9 Preservation Group	Bluebell Railway, Sheffield Park
94	80100			Brighton Std4 Tank Fund	Bluebell Railway, Sheffield Park.
95	30847			847 Locomotive Pres. Fund	Bluebell Railway, Sheffield Park.
96	5224			Privately	GCR Loughborough
97	78018			Privately	Market Bosworth.
98	3612	DEC		Severn Valley Railway	SVR Eardington.
99	6695	MAY	1979	GW Steam Preservation Group	Swanage Railway.
100	4110			GWR Preservation Group	Southall.
101	47279	AUG		S. Yorks. 3F Trust	KWVR Haworth.
102	80136			Privately	NSR Cheddleton.
103	5193			5193 Fund	Steamport, Southport.
104	7820	SEPT		Gwili Railway	Gwili Railway, Bronwydd Arms.
105	92212			92212 Holdings Ltd.	GCR Loughborough.
106	46428	OCT		Strathspey Railway	Strathspey Railway, Aviemore.
107	73082			Camelot Locomotive Society	Bluebell Railway, Sheffield Park.
108	34059			Bluebell BofB Loco. Group	Bluebell Railway, Sheffield Park.
109	7802	NOV		Erlestoke Manor Fund	SVR Bewdley.
110	35018	MAR	1980	Privately	MHR Ropley.
111	31625			Privately	MHR Ropley.
112	34027	APR		Privately	NYMR Grosmont.
113	45699			Leander Loco. Co.	Steamtown, Carnforth.
114	31638	JULY		Privately	Bluebell Railway, Sheffield Park.
115	80080	NOV		80080 Holdings Ltd.	PRS Matlock.
116	92134	DEC		Std Nine Locomotive Group	NYMR Grosmont.
117	92214			Peak Railway 9F Loco. Ltd.	PRS Buxton.
118	34067	JAN	1981	Privately	MHR Ropley.
119	4612			Keighley & Worth Valley Rly	KWVR Haworth.
120	4121	FEB		Privately	DFR Norchard.
121	75014			75014 Loco. Operators	NYMR Grosmont.
122	30828	MAR		Eastleigh Railway Pres. Society	BREL Eastleigh.
123	2885			GWR Preservation Group	Southall.
124	5532	APR		Forest Prairie Fund	DFR Norchard.
125	5972	MAY		Privately	Wakefield.
126	4936			Kinlet Hall Loco. Ltd.	PRS Matlock.
127	34007			34007 Wadebridge Group	PVR Plymouth.
128	9629			Com. Holiday Inns of Canada	Steamtown, Carnforth.
129	7903	JUNE		Foremarke Hall Ltd.	SCR Blunsdon.
130	2807			Cotswold Steam Preservation Ltd.	G-WR Toddington.
131	6634			GW Stock Fund	ESR Cranmore.
132	7821			Privately	G-WR Toddington.
133	7828			Privately	G-WR Toddington.
134	45491	JULY		W. Lancs. Black 5 Fund	Blackpool.

No.	Loco. No.	Month	Year	Purchaser	Moved to
135	48624			48518 Preservation Society	PRS Buxton.
136	5952	SEPT		GW Steam Locomotives Group	G-WR Toddington.
137	7200	OCT		Quainton Railway Society	Quainton Road, Bucks.
138	44123	DEC		London Midland Society	MHR Ropley.
139	75079	MAR	1982	Plym Valley Railway	PVR Plymouth.
140	34010	NOV		Privately	NYMR Grosmont.
141	9682			Privately	Southall.
142	35027	DEC		Port Line Locomotive Project	SCR Blunsdon.
143	35006	MAR	1983	P & O Locomotive Society	G-WR Toddington.
144	76084			Privately	N. Leverton, Notts.
145	78059	MAY		Bluebell Mogul Group	Bluebell Railway, Sheffield Park.
146	34070	JUNE		21C170 Manston Group	Richborough, Kent.
147	47406			Rowsley Locomotive Trust	PRS Buxton.
148	3803	NOV		Dumbleton Hall Pres. Society	DVR Buckfastleigh.
149	30499			Urie S15 Preservation Group	MHR Ropley.
150	4953	FEB	1984	Privately	DFR Norchard.
151	3850			3850 Preservation Society	WSR Minehead.
152	45337	MAY		26B Railway Co. Ltd.	ELR Bury.
153	34053	JUNE		Privately	Kingston upon Hull.
154	3802	SEPT		3802 Preservation Society	PVR Plymouth.
155	80104			Southern Steam Trust	Swanage Railway.
156	7229	OCT		Privately	PVR Plymouth.
157	80098	NOV		80080 Holdings Ltd.	MRC Butterley.
158	34072			Privately	SCR Blunsdon.
159	6023	DEC		BSLAG (resold)	Bristol Temple Meads.
160	35010	JAN	1985	BRE(1A) SPG	N. Woolwich.
161	4247	APR		4247 Preservation Society	CWR Wallingford.
162	80097	MAY		Bury Std 4 Group	ELR Bury.
163	92219			Peak Railway 9F Loco. Ltd.	PRS Buxton.
164	73096	JULY		Privately	MHR Ropley.
165	5199			GW Steam Locomotives Group	G-WR Toddington.
166	5526			Privately	G-WR Toddington.
167	4270			Swansea City Council	Lower Swansea Valley Railway.
168	48305	NOV		Privately	GCR Loughborough.
169	35025	FEB	1986	Brocklebank Line Rescue	GCR Quorn & Woodhouse.
170	35022	MAR		c/o Southern Steam Trust	Swanage Railway.
171	34028	MAY		Southern Pacific Rescue Group	Sellindge, Kent.
172	4248			Privately	Brightlingsea, Essex.
173	4277	JUNE		Cotswold Steam Preservation Ltd.	G-WR Toddington.
174	5552			Bodmin & Wenford Railway	BWR Bodmin.
175	34058	JULY		Privately	Bitton Railway.
176	3814			Privately	NYMR Grosmont.
177	73156	OCT		Bolton Steam Locomotive Ltd	ELR Bury.
178	6984			Privately	Bicester, Oxon.
179	4979			Fleetwood Loco. Centre	Fleetwood Loco. Centre, Lancs.
180	92207			Privately	ELR Bury.
181	30825	NOV		Privately	Brightlingsea, Essex.
182	45293	DEC		British Enginemen SPS	N. Woolwich.
183	42859			Privately	Kingston upon Hull.
184	45163	JAN	1987	Privately	Kingston upon Hull.
185	5538			Great Western Locomotive Fund	Llangollen Railway.
186	76077	MAY		Privately	G-WR Toddington.

Departure Summary

1968	1	1973	18	1978	11	1983	7
1969	2	1974	19	1979	11	1984	10
1970	8	1975	14	1980	8	1985	9
1971	6	1976	8	1981	21	1986	15
1972	10	1977	1	1982	4	1987	3

Total to date: 186

Ex Barry Locomotives By Site (1987)

	Via BR/LT/NCB	Via Woodham's Barry						
Bicester, Oxon	-	1	6984					
Birmingham Railway Museum, Tyseley	5	4	4983	5043	5080	7027		
Bitton Railway	-	4	34058	44123	45379	47324		
Bluebell Railway, Sheffield Park	16	10	30541	30847	31618	31638	34059	73082
			78059	80064	80100	92240		
Bodmin & Wenford Railway	-	1	5552					
Brightlingsea, Essex	-	3	4248	30825	92134			
Bristol Temple Meads	-	1	6023					
Buckfastleigh & Totnes Steam Railway	8	2	3803	4920				
Buckinghamshire Railway Centre	3	6	6024	6989	7200	9466	41313	46447
Caerphilly	1	1	41312					
Cardiff	-	1	9629					
Cholsey & Wallingford Railway	-	1	4247					
Darlington	-	1	78018					
Dean Forest Railway, Norchard	-	6	4121	4953	5521	5532	5541	9681
Derby	-	1	34101					
East Lancs Railway, Bury·	-	5	45337	46428	73156	80097	92207	
East Somerset Railway	3	2	6634	47493				
Eastleigh Works	-	1	30828					
Fleetwood Loco. Centre, Lancs.	-	2	4979	45491				
Glos-Warwick Railway	-	10	2807	4277	4936	5199	5526	5952
			7821	7828	35006	76077		
Great Central Railway	4	8	5224	6990	34039	35025	48305	61264
			71000	92212				
GWR Preservation Group	-	3	2885	4110	9682			
Great Western Society	8	10	3738	3822	4144	4942	5029	5051
			5322	5572	5900	7202		
Keighley & Worth Valley Railway	10	7	4612	42765	43924	47279	48431	75078
			78022					
Kingston upon Hull	1	3	34053	42859	45163			
Liverpool	-	1	76079					
Llangollen Railway	1	3	5538	7822	47298			
Lower Swansea Valley Railway	-	1	4270					
Mid-Hants Railway	1	11	30499	30506	31625	31806	31874	34016
			34067	34105	35018	73096	76017	
Midland Railway Centre	6	7	47327	47357	48151	53809	73129	80080
			80098					
Nene Valley Railway	1	1	34081					
North Leverton, Notts.	-	1	76084					
North Staffs. Railway	-	2	44422	80136				
North Woolwich	-	2	35010	45293				
North Yorkshire Moors Railway	7	6	3814	6619	30841	34010	75014·	80135
Paignton & Dartmouth Steam Rly	-	3	4588	5239	7827			
Peak Railway	-	4	47406	48624	92214	92219		
Plym Valley Railway	-	5	3802	4160	7229	34007	75079	
Richborough, Kent	-	1	34070					
Scottish RPS, Falkirk	3	1	80105					
Sellindge, Kent	1	1	34028					
Severn Valley Railway	12	20	2857	3612	4141	4150	4566	4930
			5164	6960	7325	7802	7812	7819
			34027	42968	45690	45699	46521	75069
			78019	80079				
Steamport, Southport	-	1	5193					
Steamtown, Carnforth	5	3	5643	34092	35005			
Strathspey Railway	3	1	46512					
Stour Valley Railway	-	1	80151					
Swanage Railway	1	4	6695	35022	80078	80104		
Swindon & Cricklade Railway	-	4	5637	7903	34072	35027		
Telford Steam Trust		1	5619					
Wakefield	-	1	5972					
West Somerset Railway	1	5	3850	4561	5542	7820	53808	
Purchased – still at Barry		12	2859	2874	3855	3862	4253	5668
			5967	30830	34046	34073	35009	35011
Reserved – still at Barry		15	2861	2873	3845	4115		
			5227	5539	5553	6686	7927	
			44901	48173	48518	80072		
			80150	92245				

Barry Locomotives by Class.

Cut	Class	Total Extant	via BR/LT/NCB	via Woodham's Barry
2	1366	1	1369	
	2800	7	2818	2807/57/59/74 **(2861/73)
1	2884	9	–	2885,3802/03/14/22/50/55/62 **(3845)
1	3150	0	–	
	4073	8	4073/79 7029	5029/43/51/80,7027
	4200	5	–	4247/48/53/70/77
8	4300	2	–	5322,7325
2	4500	3	4555	4561/66
8	4575	11	–	4588,5521/26/32/38/41/42/52/72 **(5539/53)
	'Hall'	11	–	4920/30/36/42/53/79/83,5900/52/67/72
4	5101	10	–	4110/21/41/44/50/60,5164/93/99 **(4115)
	5205	3	–	5224/39 **(5227)
3	5400	0	–	
4	5600	9	6697	5619/37/43/68,6619/34/95 **(6686)
12	5700	16	3650,5764/75/86 7714/15/52/54/60 9600/42	3738,4612/9629/81/82
	'King'	3	6000	6023/24
1	6100	1	6106	
1	6400	3	6412/30/35	
	'Mod. Hall'	7	6998	6960/84/89/90,7903 **(7927)
1	7200	3	–	7200/02/29
	'Manor'	9	7808	7802/12/19/20/21/22/27/28
17	9400	2	9400	9466
1	S15 (Urie)	2	–	30499/506
1	S15 (Maunsell)	5		30825/828/830/841/847
	Q	1	–	30541
	U	4	–	31618/625/638/806
	N	1	–	31874
1	WC/BB	10	34023/51	34007/67/70/72/73/81/92/105
1	WC/BB (Rebuilt)	10		34010/16/27/28/39/46/53/58/59/101
	MN (Rebuilt)	10	35028	35005/06/09/10/11/18/22/25/27
2	2MT 2-6-2T	4	41241/298	41312/313
	2MT 2-6-0	7	46441/443/464	46428/447/512/521
	5MT 'Crab'	3	42700	42765/859
	5MT 2-6-0	1	–	42968
	4F	4	44027	43924,44123/422
	5MT 4-6-0	18	44767/806/871/932 45000/025/110/212 45231/407/428	45163/293/337/379/491 Plus 45305 via Draper's Scrapyard **(44901)
	'Jubilee'	4	45593/96	45690/699
	3F "Jinty"	9	47383/445	47279/298/324/327/357/406/493
	8F	7	48773	48151/305/431/624 **(48173/518)
	7F	2	–	53808/09
	B1	2	61306	61264
	8P	1	–	71000
	5MT 4-6-0	5	73050	73082/96/129/156
	4MT 4-6-0	6	75027/29	75014/69/78/79
1	4MT 2-6-0	4	–	76017/77/79/84
	2MT 2-6-0	4	–	78018/19/22/59
1	4MT 2-6-4T	15	80002	80064/78/79/80/97/98/100/104/105 80135/136/151 **(80072/150)
2	9F	9	92203/220	92134/207/212/214/219/240 **(92245)

NOTES:-
1) Locomotives marked ** are at the time of writing, still the property of Messrs Woodham Bros.
2) Cut column indicates locomotives cut up by Woodham Bros only.
3) Extant column indicates total number of the class in existence from all sources.
4) Classes of which no examples came to Barry are not shown.

Woodham's Yard, Barry, 2nd March 1968.

Top Yard.

*73156	3803	3822	53809	30847	4942	31625
*73096	45690	7202	7200	30828	4979	30825
*73129	4983	4936	48431	2874	7027	7325
4141	5900	6960	5224	5199	5029	6634
4248	4930	2885	4953	30499	5972	5322
5051	31874	6619	30506	5239	5043	4247

189

| 2861 | 5637 | 6989 | 5080 | 2857 | 31806 | 6686 |
| 2807 | 5967 | 5643 | 5668 | 30841 | 31638 | 9466 |

Notes:-
Locomotives marked * just arrived in siding alongside Hood Road.
Locomotives at West Pond Site listed from west end.
Track 1 is Southern-most – Track 8 is Cutting Road.

West Pond Site

Track 1	2	3	4	5	6	7	8
73082	34010	4270	7927	5541	34070	92085	3862
35022	34039	5227	6984	6024	9629	42859	4156
34101	43924	4253	6990	6023	3612	47324	4110
34059	92214	7229	4920	5526	34027	47493	9682
75078	3850	34105	34007	5532t	35018	47406	4144
35027	3855	30541	34053	4588	30830	75069	9681
35029	3817	92245	80078	5193	35025	46512	4612
35010	45379	2873	80136	4561	35009	78019	3738
46521	48173	2859	7822	5521	5952	78059	
78022	48624	3814	7819	4566	7903	78018	
75079	48518	34081	7821	5539	34016	47279	
46428	92240	34067	7827	5572	34028	46447	
80151	76017	34073	7828	5538	35006	42968	
92134	45337	34058	7812	5542	3845	47298	
42765	45163	45699	7820	5553	34092		
75014	44901	44123	4277	5552	34072		
71000	45293	44422	6695	4160	92207		
47357	45491	3802	5619	4115			
41312	35005	92219	31618	4121			
47327	34046	80100	53808	4150			
	41313	80072	7802	80064			
		80150	35011	80104			
				80105			
				80098			
				80097			
				80080			
				80079			
				80135			

(Courtesy Jim Arkell)

Woodham's Yard, Barry, 10th August 1980.

Information from the foreman was that the next locomotive to be cut up – next week – would be
No. 35025 *Brocklebank Line*, followed by No. 5199 and possibly No. 48305.
The order in each siding is from the Town end.
Sidings numbered from North to South.
Inscriptions noted appear to be those current.

Cutting Up Yard: Track 1.

SR C2X tender	(Arrived 7/80)
3862 + tender	Marked as reserved Plym & Tamar Valley.
5199	Various parts marked as sold to 4121 Group. Boiler reserved for 4110 (Southall).
5972	Marked Reserved BR Enginemen 1A 18/5/80, "DO NOT CUT!".
2873 + tender	Coupling rods in situ.
5967	
4248	Coupling rods in situ.
2861	Coupling rods in situ.
30825	Boiler reserved for Mid-Hants Railway.
S15 tender	Sold to Urie S15 Preservation Group 7/80.

Cutting Up Yard: Track 2.

2807	Reserved BSLAG.
4277	Three coupling rods are lying in a pile on nearside of locomotive.
73156	Various parts reserved for Camelot Society.
35009	Reserved BR Enginemen 1A, 16/5/80.
5526	
3845	Parts of motion sold to 4121 Group. Rods reserved for 2885.
92245	
75079	Reserved Plym & Tamar Valley.

Main Yard: Track 1

GWR tender	
7200	Reserved Quainton Road.
4270	

34028	
34067	Sold to Mid-Hants Railway.
7927	Cylinders reserved for 7903.
92214	Sold to Peak Railway Society – ("who won't be happy about rear end damage during recent shunting!").
4979	Sold for Quainton Road.
Standard tender	Sold with 92214
GWR tender	
GWR tender	Sold with 4979.
7828	
5668	Reserved 5668 Fund.
9682	Reserved GWRPG.
3855 + tender	
6023 + tender	Reserved BSLAG/6023 Fund.

Main Yard: Track 2.

35025	Smokebox door reserved for Squadron Fund, and wheels for 34027.
48305 + tender	"All bottom half of loco. reserved for K&WVR – Firebox U/S". Tender reserved for BR Enginemen 1A.
GWR tender	Reserved for 2885.
44123 + tender	Reserved Fowler 3F Society.
35006 + tender	Tender sold with 34053.
GWR tender	
73096	Reserved Camelot Loco. Society.
92207	
7903	Reserved Foremarke Hall Fund.
92134	Sold NYMR 1/7/80.
4247	Reserved BSLAG.
3802	
30830 + tender	
45491	Reserved LMS Preservation Group.
34046	LH Cylinder reserved 34027.

Main Yard: Track 3.

34058	Cylinders wanted for 34027.
48518 + tender	Marked "Sold to Peak Railway Society".
80150	Reserved.
78059	Reserved Bluebell Railway.
34073	Reserved Squadron Fund. Wheels marked "Reserved K&WVR".
34053	Sold to Bournemouth Steam Centre.
80104	Reserved Wessex Loco. Society 24/6/80.
34007	Reserved Plym & Tamar Valley.
34072	Reserved Squadron Fund. Wheels marked "Reserved K&WVR".
4612	
42859 + tender	Various parts + wheels reserved AGW (Andy Wilson).
35027	Reserved Bournemouth Steam Centre. Smokebox door reserved Squadron Fund.
76077	
35011	
75014	Sold NYMR 1/7/80.
GWR tender	
80080	
80098	
4115	Wheels reserved for 4110.
45163	
45337	
44901	

Main Yard: Track 4.

30499	Sold to Urie S15 Preservation Group.
GWR tender	
GWR tender	
LMS 4F tender	
LMS Stanier tender	
4953	
3814	Parts of motion sold/reserved for 4121 Group.
6686	Springs reserved for 6634.
GWR tender	Reserved for 7903
34010	Sold NYMR.
3850	
35010	Reserved BR Enginemen 1A – also Southport.
80097	Reserved NYMR 1/7/80.
5952 + tender	Reserved Swanage 8/80.
4936 + tender	Tender reserved for 5972.
48624	"Wheels wanted K&WVR".
6634	Reserved Cranmore.
34070	Reserved Manston Loco. Group.
2885	Reserved GWRPG Southall.
48173 + tender	Two coupling rods from this locomotive are lying alongside 34073, marked reserved for 48305 Group.

(Courtesy P. Lyons)

Below: This view from the west on 2nd July 1967 shows the locomotives in the same positions as recorded in Spring 1968. The need to keep shunting the engines in order to get any out did not arise during that period. Left to right, tracks '6' to '10' on the list, being Nos. 34070, 5541 (bunker), 7927 Willington Hall and 6984, 4270, 34010. (P. D. Nicholson)

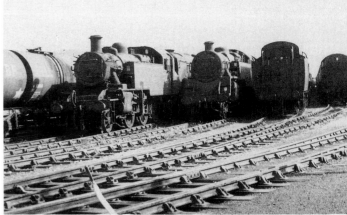

Above right: The north eastern end of the West pond site also remained unchanged from when this photograph was taken, 2nd September 1966. Left to right, tracks '2' to '5', Nos. 41313, 80135, 35011 (tender), 80079. (P. D. Nicholson)

An aerial view of the West pond site in latter days with 31 engines visible. (Courtesy D. L. V. Woodham)